OLYMPIAD WORKBOOK

INTERNATIONAL MATHEMATICS OLYMPIAD

- **01** Learning Objectives
- **02** Multiple Choice Questions
- **03** HOTS (Achievers Section)
- **04** Model Test Paper
- **05** Answer Keys and Solutions
- **06** OMR Answer Sheet

V&S PUBLISHERS

Published by:

V&S PUBLISHERS

F-2/16, Ansari road, Daryaganj, New Delhi-110002
☎ 23240026, 23240027 • *Fax:* 011-23240028
✉ info@vspublishers.com • ⊕ www.vspublishers.com

Online Brandstore: amazon.in/vspublishers

Regional Office : Hyderabad
5-1-707/1, Brij Bhawan (Beside Central Bank of India Lane)
Bank Street, Koti, Hyderabad - 500 095
☎ 040-24737290
✉ vspublishershyd@gmail.com

Follow us on:   

BUY OUR BOOKS FROM: AMAZON FLIPKART

© **Copyright:** *V&S* PUBLISHERS
ISBN 978-81-977325-0-8
New Edition

PUBLISHER'S NOTE

V&S Publishers has carved a significant niche in the publishing industry over the last decade, having successfully published more than 1000 titles across 9 languages spanning over 50 subject categories. Being known for the quality of content, we have built a reputation of excellence and reliability. We have consistently delivered **"Value & Substance"** to our readers, through a wide range of titles across a variety of genres covering school books, fiction and non-fiction that caters to different people from every section of the society.

The **Olympiad Guidebooks for classes 1-10** across all subjects, launched almost a decade ago, under the **GEN X Imprint**, became a go-to-source for the school students in no time, owing to their invaluable and substantive content written in a guidebook pattern,.

Having successfully sold a million copies of the same and in response to demand by both students as well as shopkeepers nationwide; we now present before you our newly launched **Olympiad Workbook Series**, designed for **classes 1-10 across 4 subjects**.

The workbooks are meticulously curated by a team of experienced educators, researchers and subject matter experts, edited by professionals and peer reviewed by teachers. The team has poured its efforts and expertise into creating a crisp and concise workbook which will help and guide the students to the path of success in Olympiad exams. The **MCQs** identified will not only help in scoring top marks in Olympiads but also inculcate a sense of deeper understanding of the subject, by way of solving **HOTS** and referring to complete solutions at the end of the book.

Here we present our new release– **OLYMPIAD WORKBOOK (IMO) CLASS–10** having following features:

- Based on the latest syllabi
- MCQs with comprehensive coverage of topics
- HOTS Questions liberally included
- A dedicated chapter on logical reasoning
- Model test paper for thorough practice
- Sample OMR sheet for real time simulation

We have made sure through our best efforts, that this workbook strictly follows the latest syllabi and patterns of the Olympiad Examination.

As **V&S Publishers** continuously strive to enhance the readability and maintain the credibility of our academic publications, we seek the support of our valuable readers in influencing and enriching the lives of future generations of students.

P.S. While every care has been taken to ensure the correctness of the content, if you come across any error, howsoever minor, do not hesitate to discuss with teachers while pointing that out to us in no uncertain terms.

We wish you all the best for your exams!

DISTINCTIVE FEATURES

01

Learning Objectives

They list the whole chapter as subtopics, helping the teachers to guide children in a step-by-step manner.

02

Multiple Choice Questions

MCQs act as an excellent learning aid, helping you to understand and work on your mistakes.

03

HOTS (Achievers Section)

The High Order Thinking Questions aim to help the student to solve Application-based questions and gain practical understanding of the subject.

Model Test Paper

Model test paper are provided at the end of each book, which help the student to test the knowledge which they have gained after thorough reading of all chapters.

04

Answer Key

Detailed Answer Key along with explanations aid the pupil to indentify, understand the mistakes they make during the course of Olympiad preparation.

05

CONTENTS

REAL NUMBERS

LEARNING OBJECTIVES

➤ Concept of real numbers

MULTIPLE CHOICE QUESTIONS

1. The H.C.F. of two numbers is 16 and their product is 3072. What is their L.C.M.?
   (A) 192   (B) 172
   (C) 152   (D) 186

2. What is the largest positive integer that will divide 398, 436 and 542 leaving remainder 7, 11 and 15 respectively?
   (A) 16   (B) 18
   (C) 17   (D) 14

3. The H.C.F of two numbers is 145, their L.C.M. is 2175. If one number is 725, then what is the other number?
   (A) 435   (B) 425
   (C) 415   (D) 465

4. What is the smallest number that when divided by 35, 56, and 91 leaves remainder 7 in each case?
   (A) 3847   (B) 3647
   (C) 3247   (D) 3547

5. If L.C.M. and H.C.F. of two rational numbers are equal then the numbers must be
   (A) Prime
   (B) Equal
   (C) Co–prime
   (D) Composite

6. $2 + \sqrt{2}$ is
   (A) Irrational number
   (B) an integer
   (C) not a real number
   (D) rational number

7. $1.2\overline{348}$ is
   (A) An integer
   (B) An irrational number
   (C) A rational number
   (D) None of these

8. Find the sum of the exponents of the prime factors in the prime factorization of 196.
   (A) 2   (B) 3
   (C) 4   (D) 5

9. What is the H.C.F of 95 and 152?
   (A) 1   (B) 19
   (C) 38   (D) 57

10. Find the smallest number by which $\sqrt{27}$ should be multiplied so as to get a rational number.
    (A) $\sqrt{27}$ (B) $3\sqrt{3}$
    (C) 3   (D) $\sqrt{3}$

11. If n is a natural number then $9^{2n} - 4^{2n}$ is always divisible by
    (A) 5   (B) 13
    (C) Both 5 and 13   (D) None of these

12. If n is any natural number then $6^n - 5^n$ always ends with
    (A) 3   (B) 1
    (C) 7   (D) 5

13. Find L.C.M. of 42 and 63.
    (A) 120   (B) 126
    (C) 115   (D) 116

14. What is the sum of exponents of the prime factors in the prime factorization of 576?
    (A) 6   (B) 8
    (C) 7   (D) 5

15. What is the difference of exponents of prime factors in prime factorization of 1225?
    (A) 1   (B) 2
    (C) 0   (D) None of these

16. Find the least number that is divisible by all the numbers between 1 and 10 both inclusive?
    (A) 2520   (B) 2320
    (C) 1920   (D) 2720

17. $5 - \sqrt{3}$ is
    (A) Rational number
    (B) Irrational number
    (C) Whole number
    (D) Integer

18. In the prime factorization of 13915 what is the difference between largest factor and smallest factor?
    (A) 18   (B) 23
    (C) 17   (D) 15

19. If the H.C.F. of 210 and 55 is expressible in the form $210 \times 5 + 55y$ then what is the value of y?
    (A) 19   (B) -19
    (C) 15   (D) -15

20. The decimal expansion of the rational number $\dfrac{43}{2^4 \times 5^3}$ will terminate after
    (A) 4 places   (B) 2 places
    (C) 3 places   (D) 5 places

21. The product of H.C.F. and L.C.M. of the smallest prime number and smallest composite number is
    (A) 2   (B) 6
    (C) 4   (D) 8

22. Which of the following number has terminating decimal expansion?
    (A) $\dfrac{17}{49}$ (B) $\dfrac{21}{2^3 . 5^6}$
    (C) $\dfrac{89}{2^3 . 3^2}$ (D) $\dfrac{37}{45}$

23. What is product of H.C.F. and L.C.M. of the numbers 81 and 50?
    (A) 900
    (B) 4050
    (C) 8100
    (D) 2100

24. The decimal expansion of $\dfrac{147}{120}$ will terminate after how many places of decimal?
    (A) 1   (B) 2
    (C) 3   (D) None of these

25. If H.C.F. of 306 and 657 is 9, then what is the L.C.M. of 306 and 657?
    (A) 22338   (B) 22318
    (C) 22238   (D) 22118

26. The decimal expansion of number has:
    (A) a terminating decimal
    (B) non-terminating but repeating
    (C) non-terminating non repeating
    (D) terminating after two places of decimal

27. The values of x and y in the given figure are:

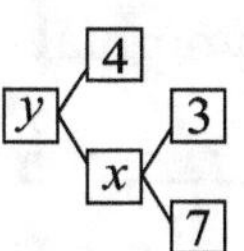

    (A) $x = 10; y = 14$ (B) $x = 21; y = 84$
    (C) $x = 21; y = 25$ (D) $x = 10; y = 40$

28. What is the greatest possible speed at which a man can walk 52 km and 91 km in an exact number of minutes?
    (A) 17 m/min   (B) 7 m/min
    (C) 13 m/min   (D) 26 m/min

29. A number $10x + y$ is multiplied by another number $10a + b$ and the result comes as $100p + 10q + r$, where $r = 2y$, $q = 2(x + y)$ and $p = 2x$; $x, y < 5$, $q \neq 0$. The value of $10a + b$ may be:
    (A) 11
    (B) 13
    (C) 31
    (D) 22

30. The decimal expansion of the rational number $\dfrac{14587}{1250}$ will terminate after
    (A) one decimal place
    (B) two decimal places
    (C) three decimal places
    (D) four decimal places

POLYNOMIALS

LEARNING OBJECTIVES

➤ Basics of polynomial   ➤ Types of Polynomial   ➤ Zero of polynomial

MULTIPLE CHOICE QUESTIONS

1. What must be subtracted from $8x^4 + 14x^3 - 2x^2 + 7x - 8$ so that the resulting polynomial is exactly divisible by $4x^2 + 3x - 2$?

   (A) $4x - 10$ (B) $14x - 10$
   (C) $2x - 10$ (D) $14x + 10$

2. Find the other two zeros of the polynomial $2x^4 - 3x^3 - 3x^2 + 6x - 2$ if two of its roots are $\sqrt{2}$ and $-\sqrt{2}$.

   (A) 1 and $\dfrac{1}{2}$ (B) -1 and $\dfrac{1}{2}$

   (C) 2 and 1 (D) -2 and 1

3. What is the cubic polynomial in which the sum, sum of the products of its zeros taken at a time and product of its zeros as $2, -7, -14$ respectively?

   (A) $k(x^3 - 2x^2 - 7x + 14)$
   (B) $k(x^3 - 2x^2 + 8x - 14)$
   (C) $k(x^3 + 2x^2 - 7x - 4)$
   (D) $k(x^3 - x^2 - x - 14)$

4. Find the zeros of the polynomial $x^3 - 5x^2 - 16x + 80$ if two zeros are equal in magnitude but opposite in sign.

   (A) $4, -4, 5$ (B) $5, -5, 4$
   (C) $4, -4, 7$ (D) $5, -5, 6$

5. If the product of two zeros of the polynomial $2x^3 + 6x^2 - 4x + 9$ is 3 then what is its third zero?

   (A) $\dfrac{3}{2}$ (B) $\dfrac{3}{2}$

   (C) $\dfrac{1}{2}$ (D) $-\dfrac{3}{2}$

6. Find a cubic polynomial whose zeros are α, β, γ such that $\alpha + \beta + \gamma = 6$, $\alpha\beta + \beta\gamma + \gamma\alpha = -1$ and $\alpha\beta\gamma = -30$.

   (A) $x^3 - 6x^2 - x + 30$
   (B) $x^3 + 6x^2 + x - 30$
   (C) $x^3 - x^2 - 6x + 30$
   (D) None of these

7. If α, β, γ are the zeros of the polynomial $2x^3 + x^2 - 13x + 6$, what is the value of $\alpha\beta\gamma$?

   (A) 3 (B) $-\dfrac{1}{2}$

   (C) -3 (D) $-\dfrac{7}{2}$

8. Find the polynomial which when divided by $-x^2 + x - 1$ gives a quotient $x - 2$ and remainder 3.

   (A) $-x^3 + 3x^2 - 3x + 5$
   (B) $-x^3 - 3x^2 - 3x - 5$
   (C) $x^3 - 3x^2 + 3x - 5$
   (D) None of these

9. What must be added to $f(x)$

   $= 4x^4 + 2x^3 - 2x^2 + x - 1$ so that the resulting polynomial is divisible by $g(x) = x^2 + 2x - 3$?

   (A) $61x - 65$

   (B) $-61x + 65$

   (C) $-61x - 65$

   (D) None of these

10. If the polynomial $6x^4 + 8x^3 + 17x^2 + 21x + 7$ is divided by another polynomial $3x^2 + 4x + 1$, the remainder comes out to be $ax + b$. What is the value of a and b?

    (A) $a = 1, b = 2$

    (B) $a = 2, b = 1$

    (C) $a = -2, b = 1$

    (D) $a = -1, b = -2$

11. What is the cubic polynomial whose zeros are α, β, γ such that $\alpha + \beta + \gamma = 4$. $\alpha\beta\gamma = -6$ and $\alpha\beta + \beta\gamma + \gamma\alpha = 1$?

    (A) $x^3 - 4x^2 + x + 6$

    (B) $x^3 - 2x^2 - x + 6$

    (C) $x^3 - 4x^2 + 4x - 6$

    (D) $x^3 - 4x^2 - x - 6$

12. Find a cubic polynomial whose roots are $-2, -3,$ and -1.

    (A) $x^3 - 6x^2 + 9x + 6$

    (B) $x^3 + 6x^2 + 11x + 6$

    (C) $x^3 + 6x^2 - 11x - 6$

    (D) None of these

13. Which quadratic polynomial has sum of its zeros as -5 and product of its zero as -12?

    (A) $x^2 + 5x - 12$

    (B) $x^2 - 5x + 12$

    (C) $x^2 - 5x + 6$

    (D) $x^2 - 10x + 12$

14. If divisor is $2 - x + x^2$ and quotient is $(3x - 1)$ then what is the dividend if dividend is completely divisible?

    (A) $3x^3 - 2x^2 - 7x + 2$

    (B) $3x^3 - 4x^2 + 7x - 2$

    (C) $3x^3 - 4x^2 - 7x + 2$

    (D) None of these

15. What are the zeros of $x^2 - 2x - 3$?

    (A) $1, -3$

    (B) $-3, -1$

    (C) $3, 1$

    (D) $3, -1$

16. Find the quadratic polynomial whose zeros are $\dfrac{2}{3}$ and $-\dfrac{1}{4}$.

    (A) $\dfrac{1}{12}(4x^2 - 5x - 2)$

    (B) $\dfrac{1}{12}(12x^2 - 5x - 2)$

    (C) $\dfrac{1}{12}(12x^2 - 2x + 5)$

    (D) $\dfrac{1}{12}(12x^2 + 5x - 2)$

17. If α, β are zeros of $2x^2 + 5x - 10$ then what is the value of $\alpha\beta$?

    (A) -5

    (B) 5

    (C) $\dfrac{2}{5}$

    (D) $\dfrac{-5}{2}$

18. The product of zeros of the polynomial $x^3 + 4x^2 + x - 6$ is

    (A) -4 (B) 4

    (C) -6 (D) 6

19. If l, m, n are the zeros of polynomial $x^3 - px^2 + dx - r$ then what is the value of $\dfrac{1}{lm} + \dfrac{1}{mn} + \dfrac{1}{nl}$?

(A) $\dfrac{p}{r}$

(B) $\dfrac{r}{p}$

(C) $-\dfrac{p}{r}$

(D) $\dfrac{-r}{p}$

20. If one zero of the polynomial $(K^2+4)x^2+13x+4K$ is reciprocal of the other, what is the value of K?
   (A) 2
   (B) –2
   (C) 4
   (D) –4

21. If α, β are the zeros of a polynomial such $\alpha + \beta = -6$ and $\alpha\beta = -4$, then what is the polynomial?
   (A) $x^2 + 6x - 4$
   (B) $x^2 - 6x + 4$
   (C) $x^2 - 6x$
   (D) None of these

22. If $f(x) = 4\sqrt{3}x^2 + 5x - 2\sqrt{3}$, with α and β as its zeros then what is the product of zeros?

(A) $\dfrac{1}{2}$

(B) $-\dfrac{1}{2}$

(C) $\dfrac{-5}{4}$

(D) $\dfrac{-5}{4\sqrt{3}}$

23. If divisor is $x-1-x^2$ and dividend is $3x^2 - x^3 - 3x + 5$, then what is the remainder?
   (A) $x - 3$ (B) 3
   (C) –3   (D) $x + 3$

24. Find the quotient if dividend is $30x^4 + 11x^3 - 82x^2 - 12x + 48$ and divisor is $3x^2 + 2x - 4$.
   (A) $10x^2 + 3x - 12$
   (B) $10x^2 - 3x - 12$
   (C) $10x^2 - 6x - 6$
   (D) None of these

25. If α, β are zeros of the polynomial $x^2 - px + d$, then what is the value of $\dfrac{1}{\alpha} + \dfrac{1}{\beta}$?

(A) $\dfrac{p}{d}$ (B) $\dfrac{d}{p}$

(C) 1   (D) $-\dfrac{p}{d}$

HOTS (ACHIEVERS SECTION)

26. If $x^2 + kx + 6 = (x + 2)(x + 3)$ for all k, find the value of k.
   (A) –1
   (B) 1
   (C) 3
   (D) 5

27. The value of $f(x) = 5x - 4x^2 + 3$ when $x = -1$, is:
   (A) 3
   (B) –12
   (C) –6
   (D) 6

28. Identify the polynomial
   (A) $x - 2 + x - 1 + 5$
   (B) $x^2 + 5\sqrt{x} + 7$
   (C) $\dfrac{1}{x^3} + 7$
   (D) $3x^2 + 7$

29. The zero of the polynomial $p(x) = 2x + 5$ is
   (A) 2
   (B) 5
   (C) $\dfrac{2}{5}$
   (D) $-\dfrac{5}{2}$

30. The number of zeros of $x^2 + 4x + 2$
   (A) 1
   (B) 2
   (C) 3
   (D) none of these

1.	Ⓐ Ⓑ Ⓒ Ⓓ	7.	Ⓐ Ⓑ Ⓒ Ⓓ	13.	Ⓐ Ⓑ Ⓒ Ⓓ	19	Ⓐ Ⓑ Ⓒ Ⓓ	25.	Ⓐ Ⓑ Ⓒ Ⓓ
2.	Ⓐ Ⓑ Ⓒ Ⓓ	8.	Ⓐ Ⓑ Ⓒ Ⓓ	14.	Ⓐ Ⓑ Ⓒ Ⓓ	20.	Ⓐ Ⓑ Ⓒ Ⓓ	26.	Ⓐ Ⓑ Ⓒ Ⓓ
3.	Ⓐ Ⓑ Ⓒ Ⓓ	9.	Ⓐ Ⓑ Ⓒ Ⓓ	15.	Ⓐ Ⓑ Ⓒ Ⓓ	21.	Ⓐ Ⓑ Ⓒ Ⓓ	27.	Ⓐ Ⓑ Ⓒ Ⓓ
4.	Ⓐ Ⓑ Ⓒ Ⓓ	10.	Ⓐ Ⓑ Ⓒ Ⓓ	16.	Ⓐ Ⓑ Ⓒ Ⓓ	22.	Ⓐ Ⓑ Ⓒ Ⓓ	28.	Ⓐ Ⓑ Ⓒ Ⓓ
5.	Ⓐ Ⓑ Ⓒ Ⓓ	11.	Ⓐ Ⓑ Ⓒ Ⓓ	17.	Ⓐ Ⓑ Ⓒ Ⓓ	23.	Ⓐ Ⓑ Ⓒ Ⓓ	29.	Ⓐ Ⓑ Ⓒ Ⓓ
6.	Ⓐ Ⓑ Ⓒ Ⓓ	12.	Ⓐ Ⓑ Ⓒ Ⓓ	18.	Ⓐ Ⓑ Ⓒ Ⓓ	24.	Ⓐ Ⓑ Ⓒ Ⓓ	30.	Ⓐ Ⓑ Ⓒ Ⓓ

LINEAR EQUATIONS IN TWO VARIABLES

3

LEARNING OBJECTIVES

➤ Linear equation in two variables
➤ Methods for Solving Simultaneous Linear Equations

MULTIPLE CHOICE QUESTIONS

1. What is the value of k for which the system of equations $3x + 5y = 0$ and $kx + 10y = 0$, has a non–zero solution?
   (A) 2   (B) 4
   (C) 6   (D) 8

2. What is the value of k for which the system of equations $3x + y = 1$ and $(2k - 1) x + (k - 1) y = 2k + 1$ has no solution.
   (A) 2   (B) –2
   (C) 3   (D) 4

3. What are the values of x and y, if
   $$\frac{a}{x} - \frac{b}{y} = 0, \quad \frac{ab^2}{x} + \frac{a^2b}{y} = a^2 + b^2,$$
   where $x \neq 0, y \neq 0$?
   (A) $x = b, y = 1$
   (B) $x = a, y = b$
   (C) $x = 1, y = b$
   (D) $x = a, y = 1$

4. What are the values of x and y, if $2(ax - by) + (a + 4b) = 0$ and $2(bx + ay) + (b - 4a) = 0$
   (A) $x = 2, y = -1$ (B) $x = \dfrac{-1}{2}, y = 2$
   (C) $y = \dfrac{-1}{2}, x = 1$ (D) $x = 2, y = \dfrac{-1}{2}$

5. What are the values of m and n for which the system of linear equations has infinitely many solutions, $3x + 4y = 12$, $(m + n)x + 2(m - n)y = (5m - 1)$?
   (A) $m = 1, n = 1$
   (B) $m = 5, n = 1$
   (C) $m = 1, n = 5$
   (D) $m = 5, n = 2$

6. The length of a field exceeds its breadth by 3 meters. If the length is increased by 3 meters and breadth is decreased by 2 meters, the area remains the same. What are the length and breadth respectively of the field?
   (A) 15 m, 12 m   (B) 12 m, 15 m
   (C) 18 m, 10 m   (D) 10 m , 18 m

7. What are the values of x and y if $x + y = a + b$ and $ax - by = a^2 - b^2$?
   (A) a, b (B) $-a, -b$
   (C) $a, 0$ (D) $0, b$

8. What is the value of k except which the given system of equations has a unique solution?
   $2x + 3y - 5 = 0$ and $kx - 6y - 8 = 0$
   (A) 4   (B) –4
   (C) 2   (D) 3

OLYMPIAD WORKBOOK (IMO) CLASS – 10

9. What is the value of k for which the system has no solution?
$$2x - ky + 3 = 0;\ 3x + 2y - 1 = 0$$
(A) $\dfrac{-4}{3}$

(B) $\dfrac{3}{4}$

(C) $\dfrac{-3}{4}$

(D) None of these

10. Five years ago, Ravi was thrice as old as Shashi. Ten years later Ravi will be twice as old as Shashi. What is the age of Shashi?
(A) 20 years
(B) 30 years
(C) 35 years
(D) 50 years

11. The sum of numerator and denominator of a fraction is 12. If the denominator is increased by 3, the fraction becomes $\dfrac{1}{2}$. What is the fraction?
(A) $\dfrac{2}{7}$
(B) $\dfrac{3}{7}$
(C) $\dfrac{5}{7}$
(D) $\dfrac{1}{7}$

12. In a cyclic quadrilateral $ABCD$, $\angle A = 2x - 1$, $\angle B = y + 5$, $\angle C = 2y + 15$, $\angle D = 4x - 7$. Which is the greatest angle of quadrilateral?
(A) 115°
(B) 120°
(C) 125°
(D) 85°

13. The larger of two supplementary angles exceeds the smaller by 18°. What is the value of larger angle?
(A) 81°
(B) 99°
(C) 109°
(D) 89°

14. Rajesh scored 40 marks in a test getting 3 marks for each right answer and losing one mark of each wrong answer. If 4 marks have been awarded for each correct answer and 2 marks been deducted for each incorrect answer then Rajesh will score 50 marks. What is the number of questions in the test?
(A) 30
(B) 20
(C) 15
(D) 40

15. A railway half ticket cost half the full fare and the reservation charge is the same on half ticket as on full ticket. One reserved first class ticket from Delhi to Patna costs ₹ 216. One full and one half reserved first class ticket cost ₹ 327. What is the reservation charge?
(A) ₹ 16
(B) ₹ 26
(C) ₹ 6
(D) None of these

16. The students of a class are made to stand in rows. If 4 students are extra in each row, there would be 2 rows less. If 4 students are less in each row, there would be 4 more rows. What is the number of students in the class?
(A) 96
(B) 106
(C) 86
(D) 116

17. If $\sqrt{2}\,x - \sqrt{3}\,y = 0$ and $\sqrt{5}\,x + \sqrt{2}\,y = 0$, then what is the sum of x and y?
(A) 0
(B) 2
(C) 4
(D) 3

18. If three times the larger of two numbers is divided by the smaller one, we get 4 as quotient and 3 as remainder. If seven times the smaller number is divided by the larger one, we get 5 as quotient and 1 as remainder. What is the smaller number?
(A) 15
(B) 20
(C) 18
(D) 25

19. The sum of two natural numbers is 8 and the sum of their reciprocal is $\dfrac{8}{15}$, which is the larger one?

(A) 5   (B) 7
(C) 3   (D) 6

20. A chemist has one solution containing 50% acid and a second one containing 25% acid. How much of each should be used respectively to make 10 litres of a 40% acid solution?

(A) 6 litres, 4 litres
(B) 2 litres, 6 litres
(C) 4 litres, 6 litres
(D) None of these

21. Taxi charges in a city consist of fixed charges and the remaining depending upon the distance traveled in kilometers. A person travels 70 km and pays ₹500, whereas for travelling 100 km he pays ₹680. What is rate per kilometer?

(A) 6   (B) 8
(C) 10   (D) 7

22. What are the solutions of the equation

$$\dfrac{x}{a}+\dfrac{y}{b}=a+b\ ;\ \dfrac{x}{a^2}+\dfrac{y}{b^2}=2\ ?$$

(A) $x = a^2, y = b^2$
(B) $x = b^2, y = a^2$
(C) $x = 1, y = a$
(D) $x = a, y = b$

23. If $\dfrac{2}{x}+\dfrac{3}{y}=13$, $\dfrac{5}{x}-\dfrac{4}{y}=-2$, given that $x \neq 0, y \neq 0$, then what is the value of y?

(A) $\dfrac{1}{2}$ (B) $\dfrac{1}{3}$

(C) $\dfrac{1}{4}$ (D) $\dfrac{1}{5}$

24. If $\dfrac{ax}{b}-\dfrac{by}{a}=a+b\ ;\ ax - by = 2ab$, then what is the value of y?

(A) $-a$
(B) $-b$
(C) a
(D) b

25. If $\dfrac{x+y}{xy}=2\ ;\ \dfrac{x-y}{xy}=6$ $(x \neq 0, y \neq 0)$ then what is the value of y?

(A) $\dfrac{1}{2}$

(B) $\dfrac{1}{4}$

(C) $\dfrac{-1}{2}$

(D) $\dfrac{-1}{4}$

HOTS (ACHIEVERS SECTION)

26. Customers are asked to stand in the lines. If one customer is extra in a line, then there would be two less lines. If one customer is less in line, there would be three more lines. Find the number of students in the class.

(A) 40
(B) 50
(C) 60
(D) 70

27. 8 girls and 12 boys can finish work in 10 days while 6 girls and 8 boys can finish it in 14 days. Find the time taken by the one girl alone that by one boy alone to finish the work.

(A) 120, 130
(B) 140, 280
(C) 240, 280
(D) 100, 120

28. The sum of two digits and the number formed by interchanging its digit is 110. If ten is subtracted from the first number, the new number is 4 more than 5 times of the sum of the digits in the first number. Find the first number.

   (A) 46   (B) 48

   (C) 64   (D) 84

29. A fraction becomes . when subtracted from the numerator and it becomes . when 8 is added to its denominator. Find the fraction.

   (A) 4/12   (B) 3/13

   (C) 5/12   (D) 11/7

30. Five years ago, A was thrice as old as B and ten years later, A shall be twice as old as B. What is the present age of A.

   (A) 20   (B) 50

   (C) 60   (D) 40

Darken Your Choice with HB Pencil

1.	Ⓐ Ⓑ Ⓒ Ⓓ	7.	Ⓐ Ⓑ Ⓒ Ⓓ	13.	Ⓐ Ⓑ Ⓒ Ⓓ	19	Ⓐ Ⓑ Ⓒ Ⓓ	25.	Ⓐ Ⓑ Ⓒ Ⓓ
2.	Ⓐ Ⓑ Ⓒ Ⓓ	8.	Ⓐ Ⓑ Ⓒ Ⓓ	14.	Ⓐ Ⓑ Ⓒ Ⓓ	20.	Ⓐ Ⓑ Ⓒ Ⓓ	26.	Ⓐ Ⓑ Ⓒ Ⓓ
3.	Ⓐ Ⓑ Ⓒ Ⓓ	9.	Ⓐ Ⓑ Ⓒ Ⓓ	15.	Ⓐ Ⓑ Ⓒ Ⓓ	21.	Ⓐ Ⓑ Ⓒ Ⓓ	27.	Ⓐ Ⓑ Ⓒ Ⓓ
4.	Ⓐ Ⓑ Ⓒ Ⓓ	10.	Ⓐ Ⓑ Ⓒ Ⓓ	16.	Ⓐ Ⓑ Ⓒ Ⓓ	22.	Ⓐ Ⓑ Ⓒ Ⓓ	28.	Ⓐ Ⓑ Ⓒ Ⓓ
5.	Ⓐ Ⓑ Ⓒ Ⓓ	11.	Ⓐ Ⓑ Ⓒ Ⓓ	17.	Ⓐ Ⓑ Ⓒ Ⓓ	23.	Ⓐ Ⓑ Ⓒ Ⓓ	29.	Ⓐ Ⓑ Ⓒ Ⓓ
6.	Ⓐ Ⓑ Ⓒ Ⓓ	12.	Ⓐ Ⓑ Ⓒ Ⓓ	18.	Ⓐ Ⓑ Ⓒ Ⓓ	24.	Ⓐ Ⓑ Ⓒ Ⓓ	30.	Ⓐ Ⓑ Ⓒ Ⓓ

QUADRATIC EQUATIONS 

(4)

LEARNING OBJECTIVES

➤ Basics of Quadratic equation ➤ Solutions of Quadratic equation ➤ Nature of roots

MULTIPLE CHOICE QUESTIONS

1. Find the values of y for the following equation:

$2y^2 - 5y + 2 = 5$

(A) $y = -\dfrac{1}{2}$ and $y = 3$

(B) $y = \dfrac{1}{2}$ and $y = -3$

(C) $y = \dfrac{1}{2}$ and $y = 2$

(D) $y = -\dfrac{1}{2}$ and $y = -2$

2. Which graph represents the equation:

$y = x^2 + 2x - 3$

(A) 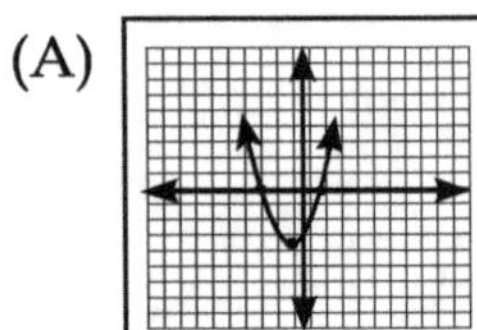   (B) 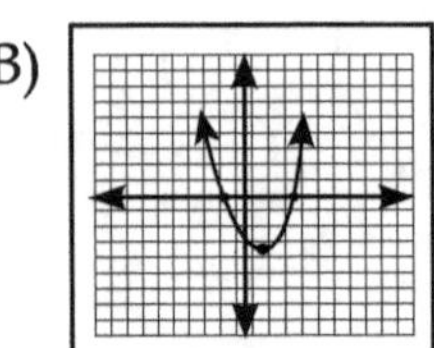

(C) 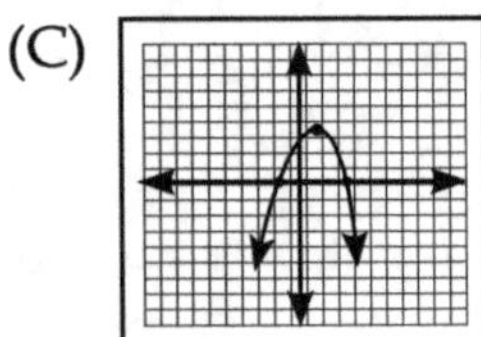   (D) 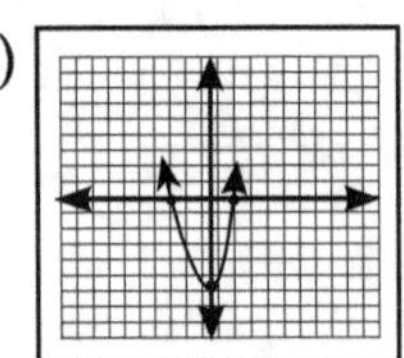

3. Use the quadratic formula to find the values of x for the equation:

$x^2 - 4x - 10 = 0$

(A) $x = 5.74$ and $x = -1.74$
(B) $x = 1.74$ and $x = -5.74$
(C) Non real answer
(D) $x = .45$ and $x = -4.45$

4. Which statement best describes the solutions to the equation below?

$3x^2 - 5x + 20 = 0$

(A) There are 2 rational solutions.
(B) There are 2 irrational solutions.
(C) There are no real solutions.
(D) There is one rational solution.

5. A ball is shot from a cannon into the air with an upward velocity of 36 ft/sec. The equation that gives the height (h) of the ball at any time (t) is: $h(t) = -16t^2 + 36t + 1.5$. Find the maximum height attained by the ball.

(A) 21.75 ft.   (B) 1.125 ft.
(C) 1.5 ft.   (D) 2.25 ft.

6. Solution set of $6x^2 + x - 15 = 0$ is

(A) $\dfrac{-2}{3}, \dfrac{3}{5}$ (B) $\dfrac{2}{3}, \dfrac{-3}{5}$

(C) $\dfrac{-3}{2}, \dfrac{5}{3}$ (D) $\dfrac{3}{2}, \dfrac{-5}{3}$

7. If $a < 0$, then function $f(x) = ax^2 + bx + c$ has a maximum value at

(A) $f\left(\dfrac{a}{2b}\right)$

(B) $f\left(-\dfrac{a}{2b}\right)$

(C) $f\left(-\dfrac{b}{2a}\right)$

(D) None of Above

8. Graph of quadratic function is
(A) circle
(B) parabola
(C) triangle
(D) rectangle

9. Quadratic function is defined as
(A) $f(x) = ax^2 + bx + c,\ a \neq 0$
(B) $f(x) = ax + bx,\ a \neq 0$
(C) $f(x) = ax^3 + bx + c,\ a \neq 0$
(D) $f(x) = a,\ a \neq 0$

10. If -5 is a root of the quadratic equation $2x^2 + Px - 15 = 0$ and the quadratic equation $P(x^2 + x) + K = 0$ has equal roots, what is the value of K?

(A) $\dfrac{7}{4}$

(B) $\dfrac{7}{8}$

(C) $\dfrac{4}{7}$

(D) $\dfrac{8}{7}$

11. If α and β are the roots of $3x^2 + 8x + 2 = 0$ then what is the value $\alpha^2 + \beta^2$?
(A) 48

(B) $\dfrac{52}{9}$

(C) 42

(D) $\dfrac{9}{52}$

12. If one root of $3x^2 + 11x + K = 0$ is reciprocal of the other then what is the value of K?
(A) 3
(B) 5
(C) -3
(D) $\dfrac{-11}{3}$

13. If the sum of roots of the equation $Kx^2 + 2x + 3K = 0$ is equal to their product, then the value of K is

(A) $\dfrac{1}{3}$ (B) $\dfrac{-2}{3}$

(C) $\dfrac{4}{3}$ (D) $\dfrac{-3}{4}$

14. If α, β are the roots of the equation $3x^2 + 8x + 2 = 0$ then the value of $\left(\dfrac{1}{\alpha} + \dfrac{1}{\beta}\right)$ is

(A) 4   (B) -4

(C) $\dfrac{3}{2}$ (D) $\dfrac{2}{3}$

15. The roots of a quadratic equation are 7 and -3, then what is the equation?
(A) $x^2 + 10x - 21 = 0$
(B) $x^2 - 4x - 21 = 0$
(C) $x^2 - 4x + 21 = 0$
(D) $x^2 - 7x + 21 = 0$

16. If the equation $mx^2 + nx + p = 0$ has equal roots then what is the value of p?

(A) $\dfrac{n^2}{4m}$ (B) $\dfrac{m}{4n^2}$

(C) $\dfrac{n}{2m}$ (D) $\dfrac{-n}{2m}$

17. If one root of the equation $x^2 + px + 12 = 0$ is 4, while the equation $x^2 + px + q = 0$ has equal roots then the value of q is

(A) $\dfrac{4}{49}$ (B) 4

(C) $\dfrac{49}{4}$ (D) $\dfrac{7}{4}$

18. If α, β are the roots of the equation $x^2 - px + q = 0$ then which equation has the roots $-\dfrac{1}{\alpha}$ and $-\dfrac{1}{\beta}$?

(A) $x^2 - px + q = 0$

(B) $qx^2 - px + 1 = 0$

(C) $qx^2 + px + 1 = 0$

(D) $x^2 + px + q = 0$

19. If α, β are the roots of the equation $x^2 - p(x+1) - c = 0$ then $(\alpha + 1)(\beta + 1)$ is equal to

(A) $1 + c$

(B) $1 - c$

(C) $c - 1$

(D) c

20. If $(a\alpha + b)^{-2} + (a\beta + b)^{-2} = 1$, where α, β are the roots of $ax^2 + bx + c = 0$ then $b = ?$

(A) $ac + 2$

(B) $a^2c^2 + 2ac$

(C) $\pm\sqrt{a^2c^2 + 2ac}$

(D) $a^2c^2 - 2ac$

21. If the difference of the root of the equation $x^2 - px + q = 0$ is unity then

(A) $p^2 - 4q = 1$

(B) $p^2 + 4q = 1$

(C) $p^2 + 4q2 = (1 + 2q)^2$

(D) $4p^2 + q^2 = (1 + 2p)^2$

22. If α, β are the roots of the equation $ax^2 + bx + c = 0$ then $\dfrac{1}{a\alpha + b} + \dfrac{1}{a\beta + b} = ?$

(A) $\dfrac{c}{ab}$

(B) $\dfrac{a}{bc}$

(C) $\dfrac{b}{ac}$

(D) None of these

23. If a, b are the roots of the equation $x^2 + x + 1 = 0$ then $a^2 + b^2 = ?$

(A) 1

(B) 2

(C) 3

(D) –1

24. If the equation $x^2 + 2x + 3K = 0$ and $2x^2 + 3x + 5K = 0$ have a non–zero common root then $K = ?$

(A) $K = 1$

(B) $K = -1$

(C) $K = -2$

(D) $K = 2$

25. If A and B are the roots of the quadratic equation $x^2 - 12x + 27 = 0$, then $A^3 + B^3$ is

(A) 27

(B) 729

(C) 756

(D) 64

HOTS (ACHIEVERS SECTION)

26. The altitude of a right triangle is 7 cm less than its base. If the hypotenuse is 13 cm, the other two sides of the triangle are equal to:

(A) Base = 10 cm and Altitude = 5 cm

(B) Base = 12 cm and Altitude = 5 cm

(C) Base = 14 cm and Altitude = 10 cm

(D) Base = 12 cm and Altitude = 10 cm

27. A train travels 360 km at a uniform speed. If the speed had been 5 km/h more, it would have taken 1 hour less for the same journey. Find the speed of the train.

(A) 30 km/hr

(B) 40 km/hr

(C) 50 km/hr

(D) 60 km/hr

28. Which one of the following is not a quadratic equation?
   (A) $(x + 2)^2 = 2(x + 3)$
   (B) $x^2 + 3x = (-1)(1 - 3x)^2$
   (C) $(x + 2)(x - 1) = x^2 - 2x - 3$
   (D) $x^3 - x^2 + 2x + 1 = (x + 1)^3$

29. Which of the following equations has 2 as a root?
   (A) $x^2 - 4x + 5 = 0$
   (B) $x^2 + 3x - 12 = 0$
   (C) $2x^2 - 7x + 6 = 0$
   (D) $3x^2 - 6x - 2 = 0$

30. The product of two consecutive positive integers is 360. To find the integers, this can be represented in the form of quadratic equation as
   (A) $x^2 + x + 360 = 0$
   (B) $x^2 + x - 360 = 0$
   (C) $2x^2 + x - 360 = 0$
   (D) $x^2 - 2x - 360 = 0$

Darken Your Choice with HB Pencil

1.	Ⓐ Ⓑ Ⓒ Ⓓ	7.	Ⓐ Ⓑ Ⓒ Ⓓ	13.	Ⓐ Ⓑ Ⓒ Ⓓ	19	Ⓐ Ⓑ Ⓒ Ⓓ	25.	Ⓐ Ⓑ Ⓒ Ⓓ
2.	Ⓐ Ⓑ Ⓒ Ⓓ	8.	Ⓐ Ⓑ Ⓒ Ⓓ	14.	Ⓐ Ⓑ Ⓒ Ⓓ	20.	Ⓐ Ⓑ Ⓒ Ⓓ	26.	Ⓐ Ⓑ Ⓒ Ⓓ
3.	Ⓐ Ⓑ Ⓒ Ⓓ	9.	Ⓐ Ⓑ Ⓒ Ⓓ	15.	Ⓐ Ⓑ Ⓒ Ⓓ	21.	Ⓐ Ⓑ Ⓒ Ⓓ	27.	Ⓐ Ⓑ Ⓒ Ⓓ
4.	Ⓐ Ⓑ Ⓒ Ⓓ	10.	Ⓐ Ⓑ Ⓒ Ⓓ	16.	Ⓐ Ⓑ Ⓒ Ⓓ	22.	Ⓐ Ⓑ Ⓒ Ⓓ	28.	Ⓐ Ⓑ Ⓒ Ⓓ
5.	Ⓐ Ⓑ Ⓒ Ⓓ	11.	Ⓐ Ⓑ Ⓒ Ⓓ	17.	Ⓐ Ⓑ Ⓒ Ⓓ	23.	Ⓐ Ⓑ Ⓒ Ⓓ	29.	Ⓐ Ⓑ Ⓒ Ⓓ
6.	Ⓐ Ⓑ Ⓒ Ⓓ	12.	Ⓐ Ⓑ Ⓒ Ⓓ	18.	Ⓐ Ⓑ Ⓒ Ⓓ	24.	Ⓐ Ⓑ Ⓒ Ⓓ	30.	Ⓐ Ⓑ Ⓒ Ⓓ

ARITHMETIC PROGRESSION

LEARNING OBJECTIVES

➤ Arithmetic Progression

➤ Arithmetic means

MULTIPLE CHOICE QUESTIONS

1. If p^{th}, q^{th} and r^{th} terms of an arithmetic progression are a, b, c respectively, then what is the value of
   $a(q-r) + b(r-p) + c(p-q)$?
   (A) 0
   (B) 1
   (C) $a+b+c$
   (D) $p+d-r$

2. The sum of three numbers which are in arithmetic progression is 12 and the sum of their cubes is 288. What are the numbers?
   (A) 2, 4, 6
   (B) 4, 6, 8
   (C) 6, 8, 10
   (D) None of these

3. What is the sum of first 20 terms of an arithmetic progression in which third term is 7 and 7th term is two more than thrice its third term?
   (A) 740   (B) 800
   (C) 840   (D) 640

4. If in an arithmetic progression the sum of m terms is n and the sum of n terms is m then what is the sum of $(m+n)$ terms?
   (A) $m+n$ (B) $2m$
   (C) $-(m+n)$ (D) $2n$

5. The first term of an arithmetic progression is 2 and the last term is 50. The sum of all these terms is 442. What is the common difference?
   (A) 3   (B) –3
   (C) 6   (D) –6

6. If the sum of first 4 terms is 24 and 12th term of this arithmetic progression is –13 then what is the sum of first 20 terms?
   (A) 200   (B) –200
   (C) 0   (D) –100

7. The sum of first seven terms of an arithmetic progression is 10 and the sum of next seven terms is 17, then what is the common difference of this arithmetic progression?
   (A) 1   (B) 7
   (C) $\dfrac{1}{7}$ (D) –7

8. If $\dfrac{b+c-a}{a}$, $\dfrac{c+a-b}{b}$, $\dfrac{a+b-c}{c}$ are in arithmetic progression then which of the following is correct?
   (A) a, b, c are in arithmetic progression
   (B) $\dfrac{1}{a}, \dfrac{1}{b}, \dfrac{1}{c}$ are in arithmetic progression
   (C) $\dfrac{1}{b}, \dfrac{1}{c}, \dfrac{1}{a}$ are in arithmetic progression
   (D) None of these

9. Find the sum of first 25 terms of an arithmetic progression whose n^{th} term is given by $7 - 3n$.
   (A) 800   (B) −800
   (C) 400   (D) −400

10. What is the sum of all three digit natural numbers which are multiples of 7?
    (A) 72336   (B) 70336
    (C) 72036   (D) 72396

11. The first, second and last term of an arithmetic progression are 4, 7 and 31 respectively. How many terms are there in the given arithmetic progression?
    (A) 14   (B) 10
    (C) 9   (D) 11

12. What is the sum of first 30 terms of the arithmetic progression whose 2nd term is 8 and 4th term is 14?
    (A) 1435   (B) 1495
    (C) 1455   (D) 1465

13. If the mth term of an arithmetic is $\dfrac{1}{n}$ and its nth term $\dfrac{1}{m}$ then what is its $(mn)^{th}$ term?
    (A) 0   (B) $m + n$
    (C) 1   (D) −1

14. In an arithmetic progression if p^{th} term is q and q^{th} term is p, then what is its nth term?
    (A) $p + q$ (B) $p - q$
    (C) $p + q - n$ (D) None of these

15. If 8th term of an arithmetic progression is 31 and its 15th term is 16 more than the 11th term of this arithmetic progression, then what is the first term of that arithmetic progression?
    (A) 4   (B) 3
    (C) −4   (D) −3

16. What is the value of k for which $5k + 2$, $4k - 1$ and $k + 2$ are in arithmetic progression?
    (A) 2   (B) 3
    (C) 4   (D) 6

17. The sum of three numbers in arithmetic progression is 27 and their product is 405. What are the numbers?
    (A) 3, 9, 15   (B) 1, 9, 17
    (C) 5, 9, 13   (D) None of these

18. If four numbers in arithmetic progression are such that their sum is 50 and the greatest number is 4 times the least, which is the least number ?
    (A) 10   (B) 15
    (C) 5   (D) 20

19. How many terms of an arithmetic progression 3, 7, 11, 15, …. are taken so that the sum is 406?
    (A) 14   (B) 10
    (C) 12   (D) 8

20. The sum of n terms of the three arithmetic progression are S_1, S_2, S_3. The first term of each arithmetic progression is unity. The common differences are 1, 2, 3 respectively, then which of the following options is correct?
    (A) $S_1 + S_3 = 2S_2$ (B) $S_1 - S_3 = S_2$
    (C) $S_1 + S_2 = S_3$ (D) $S_1 + S_3 + = S_2$

21. If the 3rd and 7th terms of an arithmetic progression are 17 and 27 respectively, find the first term of arithmetic progression.
    (A) 12   (B) 14
    (C) 10   (D) 8

22. Find the sum of n terms of an arithmetic progression whose k^{th} term is $5k + 1$
    (A) $\dfrac{n}{2}(5n + 1)$ (B) $\dfrac{n}{2}(5n + 6)$
    (C) $\dfrac{n}{2}(5n + 7)$ (D) None of these

23. If the sum of n terms of an arithmetic progression is $nP + \dfrac{1}{2}n(n - 1)Q$, where P and Q are constants, what is the common difference?
    (A) P (B) $P + Q$
    (C) $2Q$ (D) Q

24. If $S_1, S_2, S_3, \ldots S_m$ are the sum of n terms of m arithmetic progressions whose first terms are 1, 2, 3, …. m and common differences are 1, 3, 5, … $(2m-1)$ respectively, what is the value of $S_1 + S_2 + \ldots S_m$?

(A) $\dfrac{mn}{2}(mn+1)$

(B) $\dfrac{mn}{2}(mn-1)$

(C) $\dfrac{m+n}{2}(mn+1)$

(D) None of these

25. The first, second and last terms of an arithmetic progression are 5, 9 and 101 respectively. Find the number of terms in the arithmetic progression.

(A) 30

(B) 50

(C) 25

(D) 75

HOTS (ACHIEVERS SECTION)

26. Every quadratic polynomial can have at most

(A) three zeros

(B) one zero

(C) two zeros

(D) none of these

27. If $x^2 + 5px + 16$ has no real roots, then

(A) $p > \dfrac{8}{5}$

(B) $\dfrac{-8}{5} < p > \dfrac{8}{5}$

(C) $p > \dfrac{-8}{5}$

(D) none of these

28. For $ax^2 + bx + c = 0$, which of the following statement is wrong?

(A) If $b^2 - 4ac$ is a perfect square, the roots are rational.

(B) If $b^2 = 4ac$, the roots are real and equal.

(C) If $b^2 - 4ac$ is negative, no real roots exist.

(D) If $b^2 = 4ac$, the roots are real and unequal.

29. The roots of the equation $9x^2 - bx + 81 = 0$ will be equal, if the value of b is

(A) ± 9

(B) ± 18

(C) ± 27

(D) ± 54

30. Which of the following is not a quadratic equation?

(A) $3x^2 - 5x + 9$

(B) $x + \dfrac{1}{x} = 1$

(C) $x^2 - 9x = 0$

(D) $x^3 - 2x - \sqrt{5} = 0$

— Darken Your Choice with HB Pencil —

	A B C D		A B C D		A B C D		A B C D		A B C D
1.	Ⓐ Ⓑ Ⓒ Ⓓ	7.	Ⓐ Ⓑ Ⓒ Ⓓ	13.	Ⓐ Ⓑ Ⓒ Ⓓ	19.	Ⓐ Ⓑ Ⓒ Ⓓ	25.	Ⓐ Ⓑ Ⓒ Ⓓ
2.	Ⓐ Ⓑ Ⓒ Ⓓ	8.	Ⓐ Ⓑ Ⓒ Ⓓ	14.	Ⓐ Ⓑ Ⓒ Ⓓ	20.	Ⓐ Ⓑ Ⓒ Ⓓ	26.	Ⓐ Ⓑ Ⓒ Ⓓ
3.	Ⓐ Ⓑ Ⓒ Ⓓ	9.	Ⓐ Ⓑ Ⓒ Ⓓ	15.	Ⓐ Ⓑ Ⓒ Ⓓ	21.	Ⓐ Ⓑ Ⓒ Ⓓ	27.	Ⓐ Ⓑ Ⓒ Ⓓ
4.	Ⓐ Ⓑ Ⓒ Ⓓ	10.	Ⓐ Ⓑ Ⓒ Ⓓ	16.	Ⓐ Ⓑ Ⓒ Ⓓ	22.	Ⓐ Ⓑ Ⓒ Ⓓ	28.	Ⓐ Ⓑ Ⓒ Ⓓ
5.	Ⓐ Ⓑ Ⓒ Ⓓ	11.	Ⓐ Ⓑ Ⓒ Ⓓ	17.	Ⓐ Ⓑ Ⓒ Ⓓ	23.	Ⓐ Ⓑ Ⓒ Ⓓ	29.	Ⓐ Ⓑ Ⓒ Ⓓ
6.	Ⓐ Ⓑ Ⓒ Ⓓ	12.	Ⓐ Ⓑ Ⓒ Ⓓ	18.	Ⓐ Ⓑ Ⓒ Ⓓ	24.	Ⓐ Ⓑ Ⓒ Ⓓ	30.	Ⓐ Ⓑ Ⓒ Ⓓ

TRIANGLES

LEARNING OBJECTIVES

- ➤ Basics of Triangle
- ➤ Types of triangles
- ➤ Similarity of triangles
- ➤ Pythagoras theorem

MULTIPLE CHOICE QUESTIONS

1. In the given figure $\triangle PQR$, $ST \parallel QR$, such that $PS = (7x - 4)$ cm, $PT = (5x - 2)$ cm, $QS = (3x + 4)$ cm, $RT = 3x$ cm. What is the value of x?

   (A) 4
   (B) 3
   (C) 5
   (D) 2

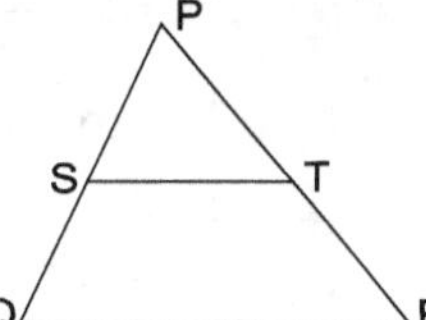

2. In $\triangle ABC$, $\dfrac{AB}{AC} = \dfrac{BD}{DC}$, $\angle B = 70°$, $\angle C = 50°$ then $\angle BAD = ?$

   (A) 40°
   (B) 30°
   (C) 5°
   (D) 50°

3. A ladder 15 m long reaches a window which is 9 m above the ground on one side of a street. Keeping its foot at the same point, the ladder is turned to the other side of the street to reach a window 12 m high. What is the width of the street?

   (A) 21 m
   (B) 20 m
   (C) 12 m
   (D) 15 m

4. In $\triangle LMN$, P and Q are the mid–points of LM and LN respectively. What is the ratio of the area of $\triangle LPQ$, and $\triangle LMN$?

   (A) 4:1
   (B) 1:4
   (C) 2:3
   (D) 3:2

5. The corresponding altitudes of two similar triangles are 6 cm and 9 cm respectively. What is ratio of their areas?

   (A) $16 : 9$
   (B) $4 : 9$
   (C) $1 : 4$
   (D) $16 : 25$

6. $ABCD$ is a trapezium in which $AB \parallel DC$ and $AB = 2CD$. If the diagonals of the trapezium intersect each other at point O, what is the ratio of the area of $\triangle AOB$ and $\triangle COD$?

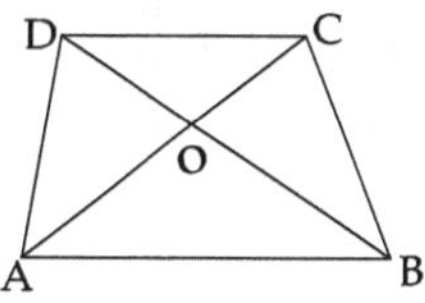

   (A) 1:4
   (B) 4:1
   (C) 1:9
   (D) 9:1

7. In the given figure, $\triangle ODC \sim \triangle OBA$, $\angle BOC = 115°$, $\angle CDO = 70°$. What is the value of $\angle OAB$?

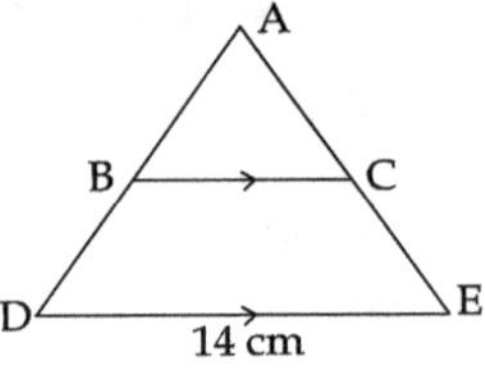

(A) 45°

(B) 65°

(C) 35°

(D) 55°

8. Two poles of heights 6 m and 11 m stand vertically on a plane ground. If the distance between their feet is 12 m what is the distance between their tops?

(A) 13 m

(B) 12 m

(C) 15 m

(D) None of these

9. A tree is broken off 6 m from the ground and its top touches the ground at a distance of 8 m from the base of the tree. What is the original height of the tree?

(A) 20 m

(B) 12 m

(C) 16 m

(D) 14 m

10. In a triangle ABC, $\angle B = 55°$, $\angle C = 35°$ then which of the following option is true?

(A) $BC^2 = AB^2 + AC^2$

(B) $AC^2 = AB^2 + BC^2$

(C) $AB^2 = BC^2 + AC^2$

(D) None of these

11. An exterior angle of a triangle measures 110° and its interior opposite angles are in the ratio 2:3. Which is the largest angle of the triangle?

(A) 66°   (B)   70°

(C) 44°   (D)   64°

12. In the figure given below, what is the measure of angle $\angle DAE$?

(A) 60°

(B) 50°

(C) 90°

(D) 80°

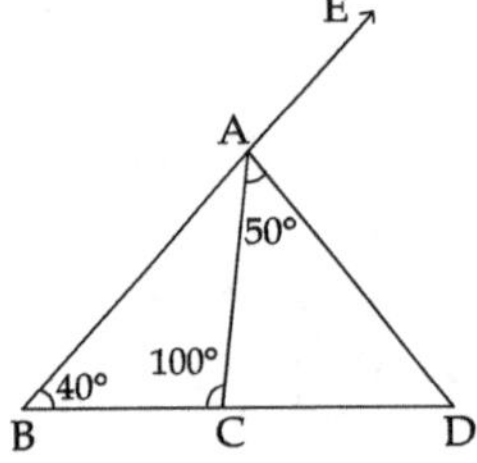

13. What is the perimeter of a rhombus the length of whose diagonal are 16 cm and 30 cm?

(A) 64 cm   (B) 68 cm

(C) 72 cm   (D) 76 cm.

14. Two isosceles triangles with equal vertical angles have their areas in the ratio 225:289. What is the ratio between corresponding altitudes?

(A) 17:15   (B) 15:17

(C) 15:13   (D) 13:15

15. In the given figure BC is parallel to DE. Area of $\triangle ABC$ is 25 cm². Area of trapezium $BCED$ is 24 cm², if $DE = 14$ cm what is the length of BC?

(A) 15 cm

(B) 10 cm

(C) 28 cm

(D) 20 cm

16.

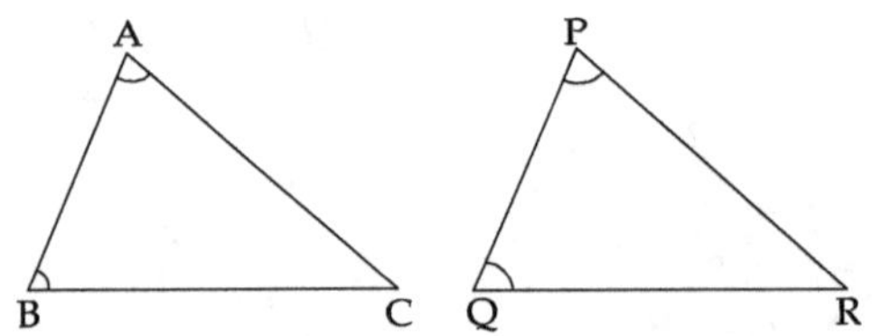

$\triangle ABC \sim \triangle PQR$ such that $\angle A = \angle P$ and $\angle B = \angle Q$ What is $\dfrac{ar(\triangle ABC)}{ar(\triangle PQR)}$ if $BC : QR = 9:7$?

(A) $\dfrac{81}{49}$ (B) $\dfrac{49}{81}$

(C) $\dfrac{81}{7}$ (D) $\dfrac{49}{9}$

17. A man goes 10 m due south and then 24 m due west. How far is he from the starting point?

(A) 26 m

(B) 25 cm

(C) 27 cm

(D) None of these

18. $\triangle ABC \sim \triangle APQ$, if $BC = 8$ cm, $PQ = 4$ cm, $AQ = 2.8$ cm $BA = 6.5$ cm, $AP = 3.25$ cm. What is length of AC?

(A) 5.6 cm

(B) 3.5 cm

(C) 6.5 cm

(D) 2.8 cm

19. A vertical pole 12 m long casts a shadow of 8 m long on the ground. At the same time, a tower casts a shadow 40 m long on the ground. What is the height of the tower?

(A) 80 m

(B) 20 m

(C) 60 m

(D) None of these

20. $\triangle ABC$ is a right angled triangle in which $\angle C = 90°$ and $AC = \sqrt{3}BC$. What is the measure of $\angle B$?

(A) 30°

(B) 45°

(C) 60°

(D) None of these

21. In an isosceles triangle $\triangle ABC$ if $AB = AC = 13$ cm and altitude from A on BC is 5 cm. what is the length of BC?

(A) 12 cm

(B) 24 cm

(C) 6 cm

(D) None of these.

22. In an isosceles triangle $AB = AC = 25$ cm $BC = 14$ cm. What is the length of altitude from A on BC?

(A) 24 cm

(B) 26 cm

(C) 12 cm

(D) 13 cm

23. The perimeter of two similar triangles are 25 cm and 15 cm respectively. If one side of first triangle is 9 cm, then what is the corresponding side of the second triangle?

(A) 5.4 cm

(B) 4.5 cm

(C) 3.5 cm

(D) 6.4 cm

24. The areas of two equilateral triangles are in the ratio 196:169. What is the ratio between their perimeters?

(A) 13:14

(B) 14:13

(C) 1:14

(D) 14:1

25. In $\triangle ABC$, AD is bisector of $\angle A$. If $AB = 5.6$ cm, $AC = 4$ cm, $DC = 3$ cm. What is length of BC?

(A) 7.2 cm

(B) 4.9 cm

(C) 6.2 cm

(D) 5.8 cm

HOTS (ACHIEVERS SECTION)

26. In $\triangle PQR$, $\angle R = \angle P$ and $QR = 4$ cm and $PR = 5$ cm. Then the length of PQ is

(A) 2 cm   (B) 2.5 cm

(C) 4 cm   (D) 5 cm

27. If $\triangle ABC \cong \triangle PQR$, then which of the following is not true?

(A) AC = PR   (B) BC = PQ

(C) QR = BC   (D) AB = PQ

28. In $\triangle ABC$, BC = AB and $\angle B = 80°$. Then $\angle A$ is equal to

(A) 40°   (B) 50°

(C) 80°   (D) 100°

29. In $\triangle$ ABC, AB = AC and $\angle$B = 50°. Then $\angle$C is equal to

(A) 40°

(B) 50°

(C) 80°

(D) 130°

30. It is given that $\triangle$ ABC $\cong \triangle$ FDE and AB = 5 cm, $\angle$B = 40° and $\angle$A = 80°. Then which of the following is true?

(A) DF = 5 cm, $\angle$F = 60°

(B) DF = 5 cm, $\angle$E = 60°

(C) DE = 5 cm, $\angle$E = 60°

(D) DE = 5 cm, $\angle$D = 40

1.	Ⓐ Ⓑ Ⓒ Ⓓ	7.	Ⓐ Ⓑ Ⓒ Ⓓ	13.	Ⓐ Ⓑ Ⓒ Ⓓ	19	Ⓐ Ⓑ Ⓒ Ⓓ	25.	Ⓐ Ⓑ Ⓒ Ⓓ
2.	Ⓐ Ⓑ Ⓒ Ⓓ	8.	Ⓐ Ⓑ Ⓒ Ⓓ	14.	Ⓐ Ⓑ Ⓒ Ⓓ	20.	Ⓐ Ⓑ Ⓒ Ⓓ	26.	Ⓐ Ⓑ Ⓒ Ⓓ
3.	Ⓐ Ⓑ Ⓒ Ⓓ	9.	Ⓐ Ⓑ Ⓒ Ⓓ	15.	Ⓐ Ⓑ Ⓒ Ⓓ	21.	Ⓐ Ⓑ Ⓒ Ⓓ	27.	Ⓐ Ⓑ Ⓒ Ⓓ
4.	Ⓐ Ⓑ Ⓒ Ⓓ	10.	Ⓐ Ⓑ Ⓒ Ⓓ	16.	Ⓐ Ⓑ Ⓒ Ⓓ	22.	Ⓐ Ⓑ Ⓒ Ⓓ	28.	Ⓐ Ⓑ Ⓒ Ⓓ
5.	Ⓐ Ⓑ Ⓒ Ⓓ	11.	Ⓐ Ⓑ Ⓒ Ⓓ	17.	Ⓐ Ⓑ Ⓒ Ⓓ	23.	Ⓐ Ⓑ Ⓒ Ⓓ	29.	Ⓐ Ⓑ Ⓒ Ⓓ
6.	Ⓐ Ⓑ Ⓒ Ⓓ	12.	Ⓐ Ⓑ Ⓒ Ⓓ	18.	Ⓐ Ⓑ Ⓒ Ⓓ	24.	Ⓐ Ⓑ Ⓒ Ⓓ	30.	Ⓐ Ⓑ Ⓒ Ⓓ

CO-ORDINATE GEOMETRY

LEARNING OBJECTIVES

➤ Cartesian coordinate
➤ Section formula

➤ Centroid of a triangle
➤ Area of a triangle

MULTIPLE CHOICE QUESTIONS

1. In which ratio does the point P (1, 2) divides the line joining A (–2, 1) and B (7, 4)?
   (A) 1:2
   (B) 2:1
   (C) 2:3
   (D) 3:2

2. The area of a triangle with vertices $(a, b + c)$ and $(b, c + a)$ and $(c, b + a)$ is
   (A) 0
   (B) abc
   (C) $a + b + c$
   (D) $(a + b + c)^2$

3. If (2, –2), (–2, 1) and (5, 2) are vertices of a right angled triangle, then the area of triangle is
   (A) 24.559 units
   (B) 12.5 sq. units
   (C) 12 sq. units
   (D) 24 sq. units.

4. Find the co-ordinates of the points which trisects the line joining (–3, 5) and (6, –7).
   (A) (2, 0) and (0, 0)
   (B) (2, 2) and (0, 1)
   (C) (–1, –1) and (0, 3)
   (D) (0, 1) and (3, –3)

5. The centre of a circle is (4, 5). $A(8, 10)$ is a point on the circumference. Find the other end of diameter of the circle through A.
   (A) (0, 0)
   (B) (0, 1)
   (C) (1, 0)
   (D) (2, 0)

6. The ends of a diagonal of a square have the co–ordinates $(a, 1)$ and $(–1, a)$, find a if the area of the square is 50 square units.
   (A) ±7
   (B) ±5
   (C) ±6
   (D) ±4

7. The ends of a diameter of a circle have the co–ordinates (4, 3) and (–4, –3), PQ is another diameter where P has co–ordinate $\left(\dfrac{5}{\sqrt{2}}, \dfrac{-5}{\sqrt{2}}\right)$ find the co-ordinates of Q.
   (A) $\left(\dfrac{-5}{\sqrt{2}}, \dfrac{5}{\sqrt{2}}\right)$
   (B) $\left(\dfrac{5}{\sqrt{2}}, 0\right)$
   (C) $\left(0, \dfrac{5}{\sqrt{2}}\right)$
   (D) (0, 0)

8. Two vertices of a triangle are (2, –4) and (1, 3). If the origin is the centroid of the triangle then what is the third vertex?
   (A) (1, 3)
   (B) (–3, 1)
   (C) (1, –1)
   (D) (3, –3)

9. The vertices of a triangle are $A(1, 1)$, $B(–2, –5)$ and $C(2, 2)$. Find the length of median through C.
   (A) $\dfrac{5}{\sqrt{2}}$
   (B) $\dfrac{25}{2}$
   (C) $\dfrac{5}{2}$
   (D) $\dfrac{\sqrt{61}}{2}$

10. What is the locus of a point equidistant from the point (2, 4) and y–axis?
   (A) $y^2 - 8x - 4y + 20 = 0$
   (B) $y^2 - 4x - 8y + 20 = 0$
   (C) $x^2 - 4x + 4y + 20 = 0$
   (D) $y^2 - 4x - 8y + 12 = 0$

11. What is the circumradius of the triangle whose vertices are (2, –2), (8, 6) and (8, –2)?
   (A) 25   (B) 5
   (C) $\sqrt{5}$ (D) None of these

12. If the co-ordinates of mid–point of the sides of a triangle are (1, 1) (2, –3) and (3, 4) what is the centroid?
   (A) (6, 2)   (B) $\left(2, \dfrac{2}{3}\right)$
   (C) (2, 1)   (D) (3, 2)

13. The sum of square of the distance of a moving point from two fixed points $(a, 0)$ and $(-a, 0)$ is equal to constant quantity $2c^2$. Find the equation of its locus.
   (A) $x^2 + y^2 = c^2$ (B) $x^2 + y^2 = 2c^2$
   (C) $x^2 + y^2 = c^2 - a^2$ (D) $x^2 + y^2 = a^2$

14. What is the value of k, so that the points $A(8, 1)$, $B(3, -4)$ and $C(2, K)$ are collinear?
   (A) 5   (B) –5
   (C) 7   (D) –6

15. If the points $(a, 0)$, $(0, b)$ and $(1, 1)$ are collinear then what is the value of $\dfrac{1}{a} + \dfrac{1}{b}$?
   (A) 1   (B) 2
   (C) –1   (D) –2

16. What is the distance of the point (4, 7) from the y–axis?
   (A) 7
   (B) 4
   (C) 11
   (D) 12

17. What is the distance between the points $(\cos\theta, \sin\theta)$ and $(\sin\theta, -\cos\theta)$ is?
   (A) $\sqrt{2}$ (B) 2
   (C) 1   (D) $\sqrt{3}$

18. If the distance between the points (3, 0) and (0, y) is 5 units and y is positive then what is the value of y?
   (A) 3   (B) 2
   (C) 4   (D) 1

19. If the centroid of the triangle formed by points $P(a, b)$, $Q(b, c)$ and $R(c, a)$ is at the origin what is the value of $a + b + c$?
   (A) 0   (B) 1
   (C) 2   (D) 3

20. What is the value of 'a' except zero for which the area of the triangle formed by the points $A(a, 2a)$, $B(-2, 6)$ $C(3, 1)$ is 10 square units?
   (A) $\dfrac{3}{8}$ (B) $\dfrac{8}{3}$
   (C) –3   (D) None of these

21. If the point $P(-1, 2)$ divides externally the line segment joining $A(2, 5)$ and B in the ratio 3:4, what is the co–ordinate of the point B?
   (A) (5, 2)   (B) (–5, –2)
   (C) (5, –2)   (D) None of these.

22. In what ratio does the y-axis divide the line segment joining the points $A(-4, 5)$ and $B(3, -7)$?
   (A) 4:3   (B) 3:4
   (C) 2:5   (D) 5:2

23. The points $A(3, 1)$, $B(0, 4)$, $C(-3, 1)$, $D(0, -2)$ are vertices of a
   (A) rectangle   (B) square
   (C) parallelogram   (D) rhombus

24. P is a point on x-axis at a distance of 3 units from y-axis to the right. What is the co-ordinate at P?
   (A) (3, 0)   (B) (0, 3)
   (C) (3, 3)   (D) (–3, 3)

25. If the point $(x, 4)$ lies on a circle whose centre is at the origin and radius is 5, what is the value of x?
   (A) ±4   (B) 0
   (C) ±3   (D) ±5

26. Find the coordinates of the point equidistant from the points A(1, 2), B (3, –4) and C(5, –6).
    (A) (2, 3)
    (B) (–1, –2)
    (C) (0, 3)
    (D) (1, 3)

27. Find the coordinates of the point equidistant from the points A(5, 1), B(–3, –7) and C(7, –1).
    (A) (2, –4)
    (B) (3, –6)
    (C) (4, 7)
    (D) (8, –6)

28. Find the value of P for which the point (–1, 3), (2, p) and (5, –1) are collinear.
    (A) 4
    (B) 3
    (C) 2
    (D) 1

29. Find the distance of the point (–6, 8) from the origin.
    (A) 8
    (B) 11
    (C) 10
    (D) 9

30. Find the value of p for which the points (–5, 1), (1, p) and (4, –2) are collinear.
    (A) –3
    (B) –2
    (C) 0
    (D) –1

	A	B	C	D			A	B	C	D			A	B	C	D			A	B	C	D			A	B	C	D
1.	Ⓐ	Ⓑ	Ⓒ	Ⓓ	7.	Ⓐ	Ⓑ	Ⓒ	Ⓓ	13.	Ⓐ	Ⓑ	Ⓒ	Ⓓ	19	Ⓐ	Ⓑ	Ⓒ	Ⓓ	25.	Ⓐ	Ⓑ	Ⓒ	Ⓓ
2.	Ⓐ	Ⓑ	Ⓒ	Ⓓ	8.	Ⓐ	Ⓑ	Ⓒ	Ⓓ	14.	Ⓐ	Ⓑ	Ⓒ	Ⓓ	20.	Ⓐ	Ⓑ	Ⓒ	Ⓓ	26.	Ⓐ	Ⓑ	Ⓒ	Ⓓ
3.	Ⓐ	Ⓑ	Ⓒ	Ⓓ	9.	Ⓐ	Ⓑ	Ⓒ	Ⓓ	15.	Ⓐ	Ⓑ	Ⓒ	Ⓓ	21.	Ⓐ	Ⓑ	Ⓒ	Ⓓ	27.	Ⓐ	Ⓑ	Ⓒ	Ⓓ
4.	Ⓐ	Ⓑ	Ⓒ	Ⓓ	10.	Ⓐ	Ⓑ	Ⓒ	Ⓓ	16.	Ⓐ	Ⓑ	Ⓒ	Ⓓ	22.	Ⓐ	Ⓑ	Ⓒ	Ⓓ	28.	Ⓐ	Ⓑ	Ⓒ	Ⓓ
5.	Ⓐ	Ⓑ	Ⓒ	Ⓓ	11.	Ⓐ	Ⓑ	Ⓒ	Ⓓ	17.	Ⓐ	Ⓑ	Ⓒ	Ⓓ	23.	Ⓐ	Ⓑ	Ⓒ	Ⓓ	29.	Ⓐ	Ⓑ	Ⓒ	Ⓓ
6.	Ⓐ	Ⓑ	Ⓒ	Ⓓ	12.	Ⓐ	Ⓑ	Ⓒ	Ⓓ	18.	Ⓐ	Ⓑ	Ⓒ	Ⓓ	24.	Ⓐ	Ⓑ	Ⓒ	Ⓓ	30.	Ⓐ	Ⓑ	Ⓒ	Ⓓ

LEARNING OBJECTIVES

➤ Basic concepts of Trigonometry
➤ Trigonometric Ratio
➤ Some applications of trigonometry

MULTIPLE CHOICE QUESTIONS

1. If in a triangle ABC, A and B are complementary, then tan C is
   (A) ∞
   (B) 0
   (C) 1
   (D) $\sqrt{3}$

2. If $\sin\alpha = \dfrac{4}{5}$ and $\cos\beta = \dfrac{4}{5}$, then which of the following is true?
   (A) $\alpha < \beta$
   (B) $\alpha > \beta$
   (C) $\alpha = \beta$
   (D) None of these

3. $\sin^2 20 + \sin^2 70$ is equal to -----.
   (A) 1
   (B) –1
   (C) 0
   (D) 2

4. $\sin\theta \cos(90° - \theta) + \cos\theta \sin(90° - \theta)$ -----.
   (A) –1
   (B) 2
   (C) 0
   (D) 1

5. A wheel makes 20 revolutions per hour. The radians it turns through 25 minutes is
   (A) $\dfrac{50\pi^c}{7}$
   (B) $\dfrac{250\pi^c}{3}$
   (C) $\dfrac{150\pi^c}{7}$
   (D) $\dfrac{50\pi^c}{3}$

6. $\dfrac{\sin^4\theta - \cos^4\theta}{\sin^2\theta - \cos^2\theta} =$
   (A) –1
   (B) 2
   (C) 0
   (D) 1

7. Simplified expression of $(\sec\theta + \tan\theta)(1 - \sin\theta)$ is
   (A) $\sin^2\theta$
   (B) $\cos^2\theta$
   (C) $\tan^2\theta$
   (D) $\cos\theta$

8. If $a = \sec\theta - \tan\theta$ and $b = \sec\theta + \tan\theta$, then
   (A) $a = b$
   (B) $\dfrac{1}{a} = \dfrac{-1}{b}$
   (C) $a = \dfrac{1}{b}$
   (D) $a - b = 1$

9. If $\sec\alpha - \tan\alpha = m$, then $\sec^4\alpha - \tan^4\alpha - 2\sec\alpha \tan\alpha$ is
   (A) m^2
   (B) $-m^2$
   (C) $\dfrac{1}{m^2}$
   (D) $\dfrac{-1}{m^2}$

10. The value of $\tan 15° \tan 20° \tan 70° \tan 75°$ is
    (A) –1
    (B) 2
    (C) 0
    (D) 1

11. If $\tan(A - 30°) = 2 - \sqrt{3}$, then find A.

(A) $\dfrac{\pi^c}{2}$ (B) $\dfrac{\pi^c}{4}$

(C) $\dfrac{\pi^c}{6}$ (D) $\dfrac{\pi^c}{3}$

12. If $\sin^4\theta - \cos^4\theta = K^4$ then $\sin^2\theta - \cos^2\theta$ is
(A) K^4 (B) K^3
(C) K^2 (D) K

13. $\dfrac{\tan^3\theta - 1}{\tan\theta - 1} =$

(A) $\sec^2\theta + \tan\theta$
(B) $\sec^2\theta - \tan\theta$
(C) 0
(D) $\tan\theta - \sec^2\theta$

14. For all values of θ, $1 + \cos\theta$ can be ____.
(A) positive
(B) negative
(C) non-positive
(D) non-negative

15. $(\operatorname{cosec}A - \sin A)(\sec A - \cos A)(\tan A + \cot A) =$
(A) -1 (B) 2
(C) 0 (D) 1

16. If $x = a\,(\operatorname{cosec}\theta + \cot\theta)$ and $y = b\,(\cot\theta - \operatorname{cosec}\theta)$, then
(A) $xy - ab = 0$ (B) $xy + ab = 0$
(C) $\dfrac{x}{a} + \dfrac{y}{b} = 1$ (D) $x^2y^2 = ab$

17. The value of $\dfrac{\cos^4 x + \cos^2 x\sin^2 x + \sin^2 x}{\cos^2 x + \sin^2 x\cos^2 x + \sin^4 x}$ is
(A) 2 (B) 1
(C) 3 (D) 0

18. $\dfrac{1}{1+\sin\theta} + \dfrac{1}{1-\sin\theta}$ is equal to
(A) $2\sec^2\theta$
(B) $2\cos^2\theta$
(C) 0
(D) 1

19. If $\tan(\alpha + \beta) = \dfrac{1}{2}$ and $\tan\alpha = \dfrac{1}{3}$, then $\tan\beta$
(A) $\dfrac{1}{6}$ (B) $\dfrac{1}{7}$
(C) 1 (D) $\dfrac{7}{6}$

20. The value of $\log\sin 0° + \log\sin 1° + \log\sin 2° + \ldots\ldots + \log\sin 90°$ is
(A) 0
(B) 1
(C) -1
(D) Undefined

21. $\sin^2 20° + \cos^2 160° - \tan^2 45° =$
(A) 2 (B) 0
(C) 1 (D) -2

22. $\dfrac{\sin\theta + \cos\theta}{\sin\theta - \cos\theta} + \dfrac{\sin\theta - \cos\theta}{\sin\theta + \cos\theta} =$

(A) $\dfrac{2}{1 - 2\cos^2\theta}$ (B) $\dfrac{2}{2\sin^2\theta - 1}$
(C) Both (1) and (2)   (D) None of these

23. The length of the side (in cm) of an equilateral triangle inscribed in a circle of radius 8 cm is
(A) $16\sqrt{3}$ (B) $12\sqrt{3}$
(C) $8\sqrt{3}$ (D) $10\sqrt{3}$

24. If $\dfrac{1+\sin\alpha}{1-\sin\alpha} = \dfrac{m^2}{n^2}$, then $\sin\alpha$ is
(A) $\dfrac{m^2+n^2}{m^2-n^2}$ (B) $\dfrac{m^2-n^2}{m^2+n^2}$
(C) $\dfrac{m^2+n^2}{n^2-m^2}$ (D) $\dfrac{n^2-m^2}{m^2+n^2}$

25. If $\sin\theta - \cos\theta = \dfrac{3}{5}$, then $\sin\theta\cos\theta =$
(A) $\dfrac{16}{25}$ (B) $\dfrac{9}{16}$
(C) $\dfrac{9}{25}$ (D) $\dfrac{8}{25}$

26. If ΔABC is right angled at C, then the value of $\cos(A+B)$ is
    (A) 0
    (B) 1
    (C) 1/2
    (D) $\sqrt{3}/2$

27. The value of $(\tan 1° \tan 2° \tan 3° \ldots \tan 89°)$ is
    (A) 0
    (B) 1
    (C) 2
    (D) 1/2

28. The value of the expression $[\text{cosec}\,(75° + \theta) - \sec(15° - \theta) - \tan(55° + \theta) + \cot(35° - \theta)]$ is
    (A) –1
    (B) 0
    (C) 1
    (D) 3/2

29. If $\cos(\alpha + \beta) = 0$, then $\sin(\alpha - \beta)$ can be reduced to
    (A) $\cos \beta$
    (B) $\cos 2\beta$
    (C) $\sin \alpha$
    (D) $\sin 2\alpha$

30. If $\cos 9\alpha = \sin\alpha$ and $9\alpha < 90°$, then the value of $\tan 5\alpha$ is
    (A) $1/\sqrt{3}$
    (B) $\sqrt{3}$
    (C) 1
    (D) 0

1.	Ⓐ Ⓑ Ⓒ Ⓓ	7.	Ⓐ Ⓑ Ⓒ Ⓓ	13.	Ⓐ Ⓑ Ⓒ Ⓓ	19	Ⓐ Ⓑ Ⓒ Ⓓ	25.	Ⓐ Ⓑ Ⓒ Ⓓ
2.	Ⓐ Ⓑ Ⓒ Ⓓ	8.	Ⓐ Ⓑ Ⓒ Ⓓ	14.	Ⓐ Ⓑ Ⓒ Ⓓ	20.	Ⓐ Ⓑ Ⓒ Ⓓ	26.	Ⓐ Ⓑ Ⓒ Ⓓ
3.	Ⓐ Ⓑ Ⓒ Ⓓ	9.	Ⓐ Ⓑ Ⓒ Ⓓ	15.	Ⓐ Ⓑ Ⓒ Ⓓ	21.	Ⓐ Ⓑ Ⓒ Ⓓ	27.	Ⓐ Ⓑ Ⓒ Ⓓ
4.	Ⓐ Ⓑ Ⓒ Ⓓ	10.	Ⓐ Ⓑ Ⓒ Ⓓ	16.	Ⓐ Ⓑ Ⓒ Ⓓ	22.	Ⓐ Ⓑ Ⓒ Ⓓ	28.	Ⓐ Ⓑ Ⓒ Ⓓ
5.	Ⓐ Ⓑ Ⓒ Ⓓ	11.	Ⓐ Ⓑ Ⓒ Ⓓ	17.	Ⓐ Ⓑ Ⓒ Ⓓ	23.	Ⓐ Ⓑ Ⓒ Ⓓ	29.	Ⓐ Ⓑ Ⓒ Ⓓ
6.	Ⓐ Ⓑ Ⓒ Ⓓ	12.	Ⓐ Ⓑ Ⓒ Ⓓ	18.	Ⓐ Ⓑ Ⓒ Ⓓ	24.	Ⓐ Ⓑ Ⓒ Ⓓ	30.	Ⓐ Ⓑ Ⓒ Ⓓ

CIRCLES

LEARNING OBJECTIVES

➤ Basic concepts of Circle

➤ Tangent

MULTIPLE CHOICE QUESTIONS

1. AB is a tangent to the circle at E. If $EC = ED$ and $\angle CDE = 62°$. Find angle $\angle AED$.

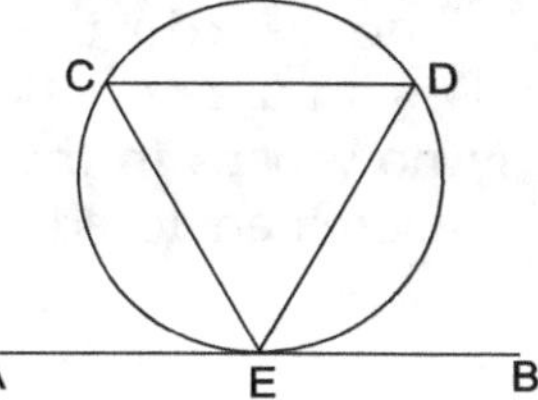

   (A) 118°
   (B) 100°
   (C) 108°
   (D) 98°

2. Two chords AB and CD of a circle intersect at an external point P as shown in figure. If $AB = 8$ cm, $BP = 10$ cm, $PD = 12$ cm, what is length of CP?

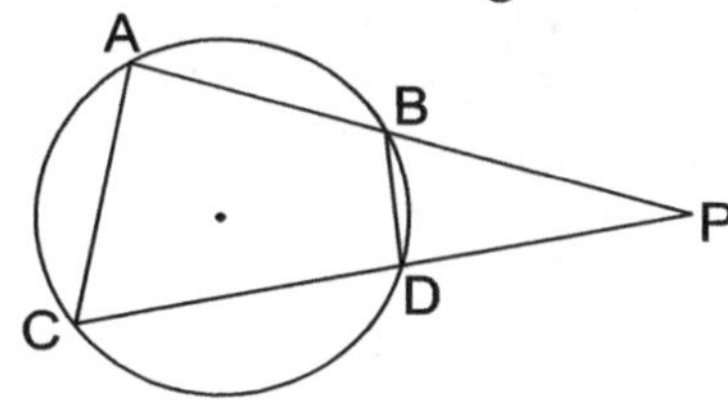

   (A) 15 cm
   (B) 12 cm
   (C) 18 cm
   (D) 10 cm

3. In the given figure AD is diameter of the circle. If $\angle BCD = 130°$. What is the value of $\angle DAB$?

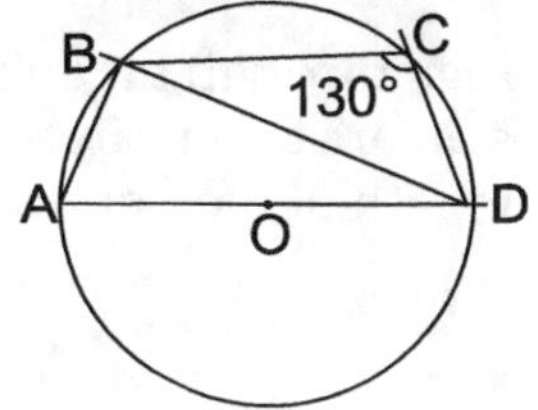

   (A) 50°   (B) 65°
   (C) 40°   (D) 70°

4. What is the length of tangent PT to a circle whose centre is at O, $OP = 17$ cm and $OT = 8$ cm?
   (A) 15 cm
   (B) 16 cm
   (C) 9 cm
   (D) 10 cm

5. What is the area of quadrant of a circle whose circumference is 22 cm?
   (A) 9.625 cm²
   (B) 10.625 cm²
   (C) 6.75 cm²
   (D) 8.75 cm²

6. The side of a square is 10 cm. What is the area of circumscribed circle?
   (A) 78.5 cm²
   (B) 157 cm²
   (C) 135 cm²
   (D) 314 cm²

7. In a circle of radius 10.5 cm, the minor arc is one-fifth of the major arc. What is the area of major arc?

(A) 288.75 cm²

(B) 281.75 cm²

(C) 271.25 cm²

(D) 262.75 cm²

8. What is the area of circle in which the difference between the radius and circumference of the circle is 37 cm?

(A) 144 cm²

(B) 154 cm²

(C) 124 cm²

(D) 224 cm²

9. A pendulum swings through an angle of 30° and describes an arc 8.8 cm in length, then what is the length of the pendulum?

(A) 16.8 cm

(B) 12.8 cm

(C) 14.2 cm

(D) 15.6 cm

10. How is the tangent at any point of a circle and radius through that point related?

(A) Perpendicular to each other

(B) Parallel to each other

(C) having same length

(D) None of these

11. The minute hand of a clock is 12 cm long. Find the area of the face of the clock described by the minute hand in 35 minutes.

(A) 252 cm² (B) 264 cm²

(C) 184 cm² (D) 1284 cm²

12. The diameter of the front and rear wheels of a tractor are 80 cm and 200 cm respectively. What are the number of revolution that a rear wheel makes to cover the distance which the front wheel covers in 800 revolutions?

(A) 640 (B) 320

(C) 240 (D) 300

13. In the given figure, $\triangle ABC$ is right angled at A with $AB = 6$ cm and $AC = 8$ cm. A circle with centre O has been inscribed inside the triangle. Find the value of the radius of the inscribed circle.

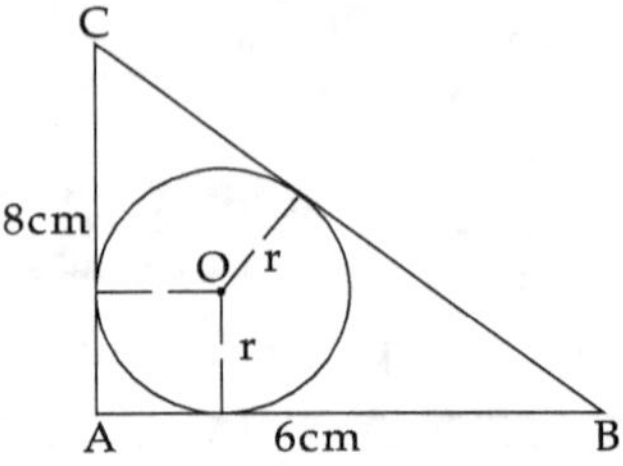

(A) 2 cm

(B) 3 cm

(C) 4 cm

(D) 5 cm

14. A copper wire when bent in the form of a square encloses an area of 484 cm². The same wire is now bent in the form of a circle. Find the area enclosed by the circle.

(A) 616 cm²

(B) 456 cm²

(C) 216 cm²

(D) None of these

15. A chord of a circle of radius 14 cm makes a right angle at the centre. Find the area of minor segment of the circle.

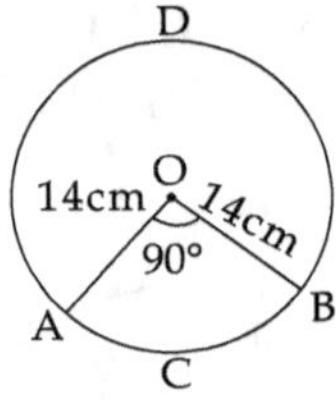

(A) 98 cm²

(B) 56 cm²

(C) 16 cm²

(D) 64 cm²

16. A race track is in the form of a ring whose inner and outer circumference are 437 m and 503 m respectively. Find the area of the track.

OLYMPIAD WORKBOOK (IMO) CLASS— 10

(A) 4935 m²

(B) 4065 m²

(C) 4135 m²

(D) None of these.

17. A field is in the form of a circle. The cost of ploughing the field at ₹ 1.50 per m² is ₹ 5775. Find the cost of fencing the field at ₹ 8.50 per meter.

(A) ₹ 1870

(B) ₹ 1670

(C) ₹ 1980

(D) ₹ 1780

18. A square park has each side of 100 m. At each corner of the park, there is a flower bed in the form of a quadrant inside the park of radius 14 m. What is the area of remaining part?

(A) 9384 m²

(B) 9684 m²

(C) 9224 m²

(D) 9386 m²

19. What is the area of shaded region if *ABCD* is a square of side 14 cm and *APD* and *BPC* are semi circles?

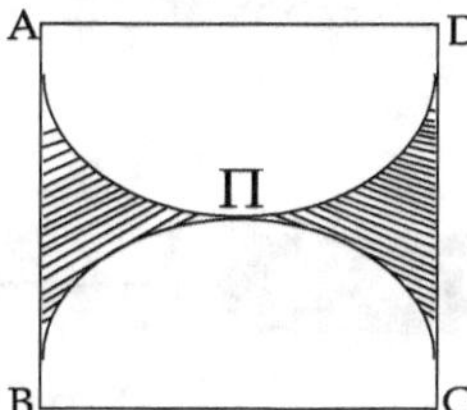

(A) 52 cm²

(B) 32 cm²

(C) 42 cm²

(D) 62 cm²

20. If the area of a sector of a circle is $\frac{7}{20}$ of the area of that circle, then what is the sector angle of the circle?

(A) 126°

(B) 130°

(C) 110°

(D) 120°

21. If the perimeter of a circle is equal to that of square, then what is the ratio of their areas?

(A) 11 : 14

(B) 22 : 13

(C) 14 : 11

(D) 13 : 22

22. The perimeter of a sector of a circle of radius 5.2 cm is 16.4 cm, then what is area of sector?

(A) 14.6 cm²

(B) 15.6 cm²

(C) 19.6 cm²

(D) None of these

23. A car has wheels which are 80 cm in diameter. How many complete revolutions does each wheel make in 10 minutes when the car is travelling at a speed of 66 kmph?

(A) 4375

(B) 4125

(C) 4275

(D) 4325

24. A bicycle wheel makes 5000 revolutions in moving 11 km. What is the radius of the wheel?

(A) 45 cm

(B) 25 cm

(C) 35 cm

(D) None of these

25. If an isosceles triangle *PQR* in which *PQ* = *PR* = 6 cm is inscribed in a circle of radius 9 cm, what is the area of triangle?

(A) $56\sqrt{2}\,\text{cm}^2$

(B) $8\sqrt{2}\,\text{cm}^2$

(C) $7\sqrt{2}\,\text{cm}^2$

(D) $9\sqrt{2}\,\text{cm}^2$

26. What is the length of tangent drawn from a point whose distance from the centre of

a circle is 25 cm, if radius of the circle is 7 cm?

(A) 24 cm   (B) 25 cm

(C) 26 cm   (D) 30 cm

27. What is the area of the fig if the radius of bigger semi-circle be 14 cm?

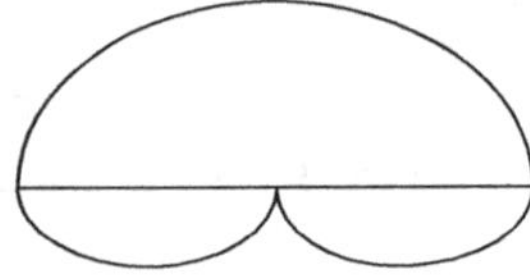

(A) 264 cm²

(B) 462 cm²

(C) 468 cm²

(D) None of these

28. A bucket is raised from a well by means of a rope which is wound round a wheel of diameter 77 cm. Given that the bucket ascends in 1 minute 28 seconds with a uniform speed of 1.1 m/s. What is the number of complete revolutions the wheel makes in raising the bucket?

(A) 60

(B) 50

(C) 30

(D) 40

29. What is the value of x in the given figure if it is given that $AB \parallel CD$?

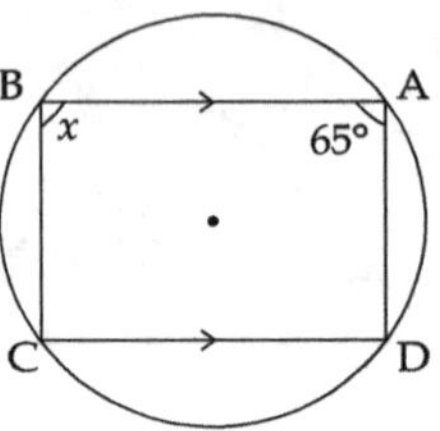

(A) 65°

(B) 115°

(C) 130°

(D) None of these

30. What is the value of y and x respectively in the given figure?

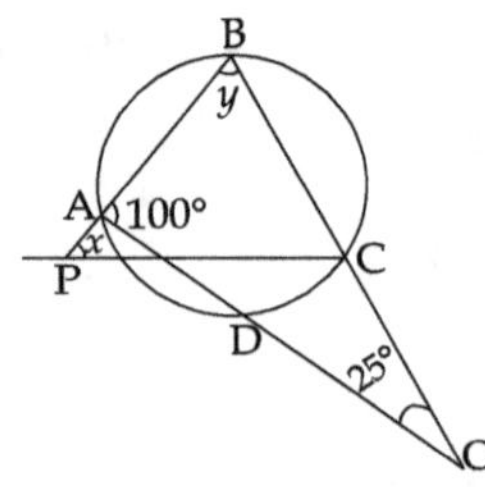

(A) $x = 55°, y = 45°$

(B) $x = 45°, y = 55°$

(C) $x = 65°, y = 55°$

(D) $x = 55°, y = 65°$

HOTS (ACHIEVERS SECTION)

31. If TP and TQ are the two tangents to a circle with centre O so that $\angle POQ = 110°$, then $\angle PTQ$ is equal to

(A) 60°

(B) 70°

(C) 80°

(D) 90°

32. Two concentric circles are of radii 5 cm and 3 cm. The length of the chord of the larger circle which touches the smaller circle is:

(A) 8 cm   (B) 10 cm

(C) 12 cm   (D) 18 cm

33. In the figure, PQL and PRM are tangents to the circle with centre O at the points Q and R, respectively and S is a point on the circle such that $\angle SQL = 50°$ and $\angle SRM = 60°$. Then $\angle QSR$ is equal to

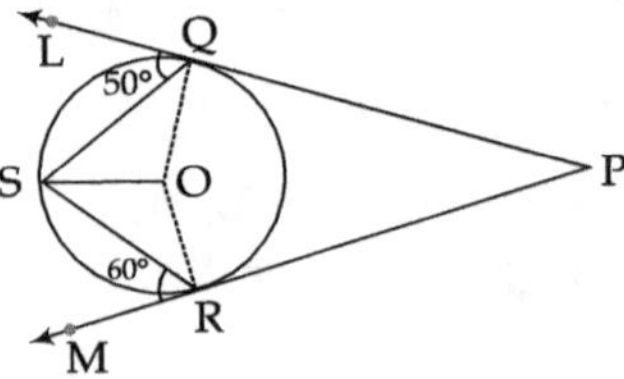

(A) 40°   (B) 60°

(C) 70°   (D) 80°

34. From a point P which is at a distance of 13 cm from the centre O of a circle of radius 5 cm, the pair of tangents PQ and PR to the circle are drawn. Then the area of the quadrilateral PQOR is

(A) 60 cm² (B) 65 cm²

(C) 30 cm² (D) 32.5 cm²

35. From a point P which is at a distance of 13 cm from the centre O of a circle of radius 5 cm, the pair of tangents PQ and PR to the circle are drawn. Then the area of the quadrilateral PQOR is

(A) 60 cm² (B) 65 cm²

(C) 30 cm² (D) 32.5 cm²

---

1. Ⓐ Ⓑ Ⓒ Ⓓ	8. Ⓐ Ⓑ Ⓒ Ⓓ	15. Ⓐ Ⓑ Ⓒ Ⓓ	22 Ⓐ Ⓑ Ⓒ Ⓓ	29. Ⓐ Ⓑ Ⓒ Ⓓ
2. Ⓐ Ⓑ Ⓒ Ⓓ	9. Ⓐ Ⓑ Ⓒ Ⓓ	16. Ⓐ Ⓑ Ⓒ Ⓓ	23. Ⓐ Ⓑ Ⓒ Ⓓ	30. Ⓐ Ⓑ Ⓒ Ⓓ
3. Ⓐ Ⓑ Ⓒ Ⓓ	10. Ⓐ Ⓑ Ⓒ Ⓓ	17. Ⓐ Ⓑ Ⓒ Ⓓ	24. Ⓐ Ⓑ Ⓒ Ⓓ	31. Ⓐ Ⓑ Ⓒ Ⓓ
4. Ⓐ Ⓑ Ⓒ Ⓓ	11. Ⓐ Ⓑ Ⓒ Ⓓ	18. Ⓐ Ⓑ Ⓒ Ⓓ	25. Ⓐ Ⓑ Ⓒ Ⓓ	32. Ⓐ Ⓑ Ⓒ Ⓓ
5. Ⓐ Ⓑ Ⓒ Ⓓ	12. Ⓐ Ⓑ Ⓒ Ⓓ	19. Ⓐ Ⓑ Ⓒ Ⓓ	26. Ⓐ Ⓑ Ⓒ Ⓓ	33. Ⓐ Ⓑ Ⓒ Ⓓ
6. Ⓐ Ⓑ Ⓒ Ⓓ	13. Ⓐ Ⓑ Ⓒ Ⓓ	20. Ⓐ Ⓑ Ⓒ Ⓓ	27. Ⓐ Ⓑ Ⓒ Ⓓ	34. Ⓐ Ⓑ Ⓒ Ⓓ
7. Ⓐ Ⓑ Ⓒ Ⓓ	14. Ⓐ Ⓑ Ⓒ Ⓓ	21. Ⓐ Ⓑ Ⓒ Ⓓ	28. Ⓐ Ⓑ Ⓒ Ⓓ	35. Ⓐ Ⓑ Ⓒ Ⓓ

SURFACE AREA AND VOLUME

LEARNING OBJECTIVES

➤ Surface Area and Volume of Cubes, Cuboids, Cylinders, Spheres and Cones

MULTIPLE CHOICE QUESTIONS

1. A solid cylinder of diameter 12 cm and height 15 cm is melted and recast into 12 toys in the shape of a right circular cone mounted on a hemisphere. Find the radius of the hemisphere, if height of the cone is 3 times the radius.
   (A) 3 cm (B) 6 cm
   (C) 5 cm (D) 9 cm

2. The surface area of a cylinder is 2992 cm^2 and its height is 20 cm, what is the diameter of the cylinder?
   (A) 14 cm (B) 28 cm
   (C) 7 cm (D) 56 cm

3. The volume of a cube is 1728 cm^3. What is the total surface area of the cube?
   (A) 824 cm^2
   (B) 864 cm^2
   (C) 924 cm^2
   (D) None of these

4. The curved surface area of a cylindrical pillar is 264 m^2 and its volume is 924 m^3. What is the height of pillar?
   (A) 4 m (B) 5 m
   (C) 6 m (D) 7 m

5. A circus tent is cylindrical to a height of 4 m and cone above it. If its diameter is 105 m and its slant height is 40 m, what is the total area of canvas required?
   (A) 1760 m^2 (B) 3960 m^2
   (C) 7920 m^2 (D) 2640 m^2

6. A solid iron hemisphere is melted and a number of solid iron balls of equal size are made. The radius of each ball is one-fourth the radius of the hemisphere. What are the number of balls that can be made?
   (A) 32 (B) 16
   (C) 64 (D) 30

7. A right cylinder, a right cone and a hemisphere have the same height and same base area. What is the ratio of their volumes?
   (A) $1 : 2 : 3$
   (B) $3 : 1 : 2$
   (C) $2 : 3 : 1$
   (D) None of these

8. A solid copper sphere of radius 10.5 cm is melted and right cones of radius 3.5 cm and height 3 cm are made from the material. What is the number of cones made?
   (A) 136 (B) 126
   (C) 156 (D) 146

9. The height of a right cylinder is 16 cm and the diameter of its base is 24 cm. Find the radius of the sphere whose volume is equal to the volume of the given cylinder.
   (A) 12 cm (B) 6 cm
   (C) 16 cm (D) 24 cm

10. The weight of a metallic spherical shell is 11.176 kg. If the inner radius of the cell is 6 cm and 1 cm³ of the metal weights 21 g then what is the thickness of the shell?

(A) 1 cm   (B) 2 cm
(C) 3 cm   (D) 4 cm

11. If the radius of a sphere is doubled then by how many times will its surface area increase?

(A) 8   (B) 4
(C) 2   (D) 0.5

12. The ratio of the volumes of two spheres is 27 : 8. Find the ratio of their surface areas.

(A) $4:9$ (B) $9:4$
(C) $2:3$ (D) $1:3$

13. The inner and outer surface area of a spherical shell are 324 πcm² and 576 πcm². What is the thickness of the shell?

(A) 6 cm   (B) 3 cm
(C) 2 cm   (D) 4 cm

14. The surface area of a sphere is 616 cm², what is the diameter of the sphere?

(A) 7 cm   (B) 14 cm
(C) 16 cm   (D) 24 cm

15. Five people can live in a tent. If each person requires 16 m² of floor area and 100 m³ space for air then find the required height of the cone of the smallest size to accommodate those people.

(A) 18.75 m   (B) 20 m
(C) 21.75 m   (D) None of these

16. The ratio of curved surface area of two right cones of equal base is 5 : 4. What is the ratio of their slant heights?

(A) $5:4$ (B) $4:5$
(C) $1:4$ (D) $1:5$

17. The ratio of the heights of two right cones is 3 : 2. Ratio of their radii of the base is 2 : 3. What is the ratio of their volumes?

(A) $2:3$ (B) $3:2$
(C) $3:1$ (D) $1:3$

18. The radius of the base of right cone is 7 cm and its height is 24 cm. What is the total surface area?

(A) 704 cm²   (B) 550 cm²
(C) 599 cm²   (D) None of these

19. The total surface area of a right cone is 1760 cm² and radius of its base is 14 cm. What is the lateral surface area of the cone?

(A) 1148 cm²   (B) 1144 cm²
(C) 1198 cm²   (D) None of these

20. The height of a conical tent is 14 m and its floor area is 346.5 m². How much canvas 1.1 m wide will be required for it?

(A) 525 m   (B) 860 m
(C) 665 m   (D) 425 cm

21. On increasing the radius of the base and the height of a cone by 20% each, by what percent will its volume be increased?

(A) 72.8%   (B) 60%
(C) 40%   (D) 30%

22. The volume of a hemisphere is 19404 cm³. What is the total surface area of the hemisphere?

(A) 4158 cm²   (B) 3696 cm²
(C) 8316 cm²   (D) 4996 cm²

23. The ratio between the volumes of two spheres is 125 : 216. What is the ratio between their surface area?

(A) $2:3$ (B) $4:5$
(C) $5:6$ (D) $25:36$

24. The radii of two cylinders are in the ratio 2 : 3 and their heights are in the ratio 5 : 3. What is the ratio of their volumes?

(A) $20:27$ (B) $27:20$
(C) $9:4$ (D) $4:9$

25. The areas of three adjacent faces of a cuboid are x, y, z respectively then the volume of the cuboid is

(A) xyz (B) $\sqrt{xyz}$
(C) $2xyz$ (D) $3\sqrt{xyz}$

26. If a solid, cone of base radius 'r' and height 'h' is placed over a solid cylinder having same base radius 'r' and height – 'h' as that of the cone, then the curved surface area of the shape is $\pi r\left(\sqrt{h^2 + r^2}\right) + 2\pi rh$. Is it true?

    (A) No
    (B) Yes
    (C) May be
    (D) Cannot be determined

27. A cylinder and a cone are of the same base radius and same height. Find the ratio of the volumes of the cylinder of that of the cone.

    (A) $1:3$ (B) $1:2$
    (C) $3:1$ (D) $2:1$

28. In the figure, the shape of a solid copper piece (made of two pieces) with dimensions as shown. The face ABCDEFA has uniform cross section. Assume that the angles at A, B, C, D, E and F are right angles. Calculate the volume of the piece.

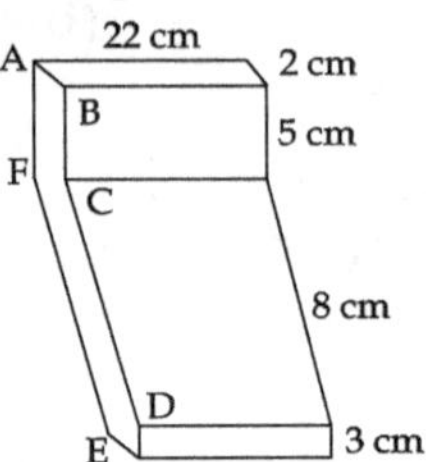

    (A) 840 cm   (B) 880 cm³
    (C) 876 cm³   (D) 890 cm³

29. A toy is in the form of a cone mounted on a hemisphere of common base radius 7 cm. The total height of the toy is 31 cm. Find the total surface area of the toy.

    (A) 465   (B) 912
    (C) 769   (D) 858

30. What is the area of a semi–circle of radius 5 cm?

    (A) 78.57 cm   (B) 71.42 cm
    (C) 63.18 cm   (D) 79.86 cm

Darken Your Choice with HB Pencil

1.	A B C D	7.	A B C D	13.	A B C D	19	A B C D	25.	A B C D
2.	A B C D	8.	A B C D	14.	A B C D	20.	A B C D	26.	A B C D
3.	A B C D	9.	A B C D	15.	A B C D	21.	A B C D	27.	A B C D
4.	A B C D	10.	A B C D	16.	A B C D	22.	A B C D	28.	A B C D
5.	A B C D	11.	A B C D	17.	A B C D	23.	A B C D	29.	A B C D
6.	A B C D	12.	A B C D	18.	A B C D	24.	A B C D	30.	A B C D

STATISTICS

LEARNING OBJECTIVES

➤ Mean ➤ Median ➤ Mode

MULTIPLE CHOICE QUESTIONS

1. If the mean of 6, 7, x, 8, y, 14 is 9, then which of the following is correct?
   (A) $x + y = 21$
   (B) $x - y = 19$
   (C) $x + y = 19$
   (D) $x - y = 21$

2. If the arithmetic mean of x, $x + 3$, $x + 6$, $x + 9$, $x + 12$ is 10 then what is the value of x.
   (A) 58 (B) 5
   (C) 6 (D) 4

3. In the following distribution.

Class	5–10	10–15	15–20	20–25	25–30	30–35	35–40	40–45
Frequency	5	6	15	10	5	4	2	2

   What is the cumulative frequency of 25–30?
   (A) 26 (B) 36
   (C) 41 (D) 45

4. In the given distribution, which is the modal class?

Class	0–10	10–20	20–30	30–40	40–50
Frequency	6	10	12	32	20

   (A) 0–10 (B) 40–50
   (C) 30–40 (D) 20–30

5. Find the median of the following data:
   20, 25, 17, 18, 8, 15, 9, 11, 14, 22
   (A) 16 (B) 12
   (C) 18 (D) 17

6. What is the value of P, if the mean of the following distribution is 7.5?

x	3	5	7	9	11	13
f	6	8	15	P	8	4

   (A) 3 (B) 6
   (C) 5 (D) 7

7. Find the median of the following data

Class	0–10	10–30	30–60	60–80	80–90
Frequency	5	15	30	8	2

   (A) 30 (B) 40
   (C) 35 (D) 45

8. The median of the given data
   41, 43, 127, 99, 61, 71, 92, 58, 57, is 61.
   If 58 is replaced by 85, then what is difference between the new median and the given median?
   (A) 9 (B) 8
   (C) 10 (D) 12

9. The number of problems worked out by a student on seven days of a week are 5, 9, 15, 11, 13, 17, 7, then what is the sum of lower quartile and upper quartile?
   (A) 15
   (B) 18
   (C) 22
   (D) 19

10. What is the interquartile range for the data

2, 1, 0, 3, 1, 2, 3, 4, 3, 5?

(A) 1   (B) 2

(C) 3   (D) 4

11. What is difference of mean and median of the following data?

Variate	2	4	6	8	10	12	14	16
Frequency	5	8	10	13	4	12	6	2

(A) 1.23

(B) 0.43

(C) 2.43

(D) 2

12. If the mean of first n natural number is 15, what is the value of n?

(A) 29

(B) 30

(C) 15

(D) 14

13. The arithmetic mean and mode of a data are 24 and 12 respectively. What is the median of that data?

(A) 18

(B) 20

(C) 23

(D) 22

14. If the mean of a frequency distribution is 8.1 and $\Sigma fx_i = 132 + 5k$, $\Sigma f_i = 20$, then what is the value of k?

(A) 5   (B) 6

(C) 7   (D) 8

15. The numbers 25, 31, $x - 3$, 37, $x + 4$, 42, 43, 45, 46 are in ascending order and their median is 39. What is the number x?

(A) 40   (B) 35

(C) 32   (D) 42

16. What is the median of the possible values of x such that $1 \leq x \leq 7$, where x is an integer?

(A) 4   (B) 3

(C) 5   (D) 4.5

17. The median of first five natural numbers is 3. If 6 is included. then what is the median. Also find the difference of the two medians?

(A) 3.5, 0.5   (B) 4, 1

(C) 4.5, 1.5   (D) None of these

18. What is the mode of the given data?

Variate	12	13	14	15	16	17	18
Frequency	21	8	9	51	38	12	25

(A) 12   (B) 16

(C) 15   (D) 18

19. What is the mean, median, mode of the following data respectively?

0, 2, 2, 3, 3, 3, 4, 5, 5, 5, 5, 6, 6, 7, 8, 8

(A) 4.5, 5, 5   (B) 5, 4, 5

(C) 5, 5, 6   (D) 4.5, 6, 6

20. What is the difference between mean and mode of the data?

3, 1, 5, 6, 3, 4, 5, 3, 7, 2

(A) 0.5   (B) 0.9

(C) 0.8   (D) 0.6

21. What is the mean of the following data?

Class Interval	0–50	50–100	100–150	150–200	200–250	250–300
Frequency	4	8	16	13	6	3

(A) 145   (B) 144

(C) 143   (D) 148

22. If the mean of the given data is 7.5 then what is the value of f?

Variable	5	6	7	8	9	10	11	12
Frequency	20	17	f	10	8	6	7	6

(A) 12   (B) 14

(C) 15   (D) 16

23. What is the median of the following distribution?

Variate	1	2	3	4	5	6	7	8	9
Frequency	8	10	11	16	20	25	15	9	6

(A) 7   (B) 6

(C) 5   (D) 4

24. What is the median of the given data?

Marks	0–10	10–20	20–30	30–40	40–50	50–60
No. of students	5	8	20	15	7	5

(A) 28.5   (B) 27.5
(C) 26.5   (D) 29.5

25. What is the mode of the following distribution?

Class	3–6	6–9	9–12	12–15	15–18	18–21	21–24
Frequency	2	5	10	23	21	12	3

(A) 14.6   (B) 15.6
(C) 12.6   (D) 13.6

HOTS (ACHIEVERS SECTION)

26. What should be the modal class?

Marks	Number of students
Below 10	3
Below 20	12
Below 30	27
Below 40	57
Below 50	75
Below 60	80

(A) 15-60   (B) 30-40
(C) 20-30   (D) 10-20

27. What should be the modal class?

Classes	0-10	10-20	20-30	30-40	40-50	50-60
Frequencies	5	6	13	38	30	4

(A) 10-20   (B) 30-40
(C) 40-50   (D) 50-60

28. What should be the frequency of 30-40 in this case?

Marks obtained	Number of students
More than or equal to 0	63
More than or equal to 10	58
More than or equal to 20	55
More than or equal to 30	51
More than or equal to 40	48
More than or equal to 50	42

(A) 51   (B) 48
(C) 4   (D) 3

29. What should be the modal class?

Classes	Frequencies
0-10	12
10-20	16
20-30	17
30-40	13
40-50	11
50-60	19

(A) 0-10   (B) 10-20
(C) 20-30   (D) 50-60

30. The abscissa of the point of interaction of the 'less than type' and of the 'more than type' cumulative frequency curve of grouped data gives
(A) Mode
(B) Median
(C) Mean
(D) All of the above

—Darken Your Choice with HB Pencil—

1.	Ⓐ Ⓑ Ⓒ Ⓓ	7.	Ⓐ Ⓑ Ⓒ Ⓓ	13.	Ⓐ Ⓑ Ⓒ Ⓓ	19	Ⓐ Ⓑ Ⓒ Ⓓ	25.	Ⓐ Ⓑ Ⓒ Ⓓ
2.	Ⓐ Ⓑ Ⓒ Ⓓ	8.	Ⓐ Ⓑ Ⓒ Ⓓ	14.	Ⓐ Ⓑ Ⓒ Ⓓ	20.	Ⓐ Ⓑ Ⓒ Ⓓ	26.	Ⓐ Ⓑ Ⓒ Ⓓ
3.	Ⓐ Ⓑ Ⓒ Ⓓ	9.	Ⓐ Ⓑ Ⓒ Ⓓ	15.	Ⓐ Ⓑ Ⓒ Ⓓ	21.	Ⓐ Ⓑ Ⓒ Ⓓ	27.	Ⓐ Ⓑ Ⓒ Ⓓ
4.	Ⓐ Ⓑ Ⓒ Ⓓ	10.	Ⓐ Ⓑ Ⓒ Ⓓ	16.	Ⓐ Ⓑ Ⓒ Ⓓ	22.	Ⓐ Ⓑ Ⓒ Ⓓ	28.	Ⓐ Ⓑ Ⓒ Ⓓ
5.	Ⓐ Ⓑ Ⓒ Ⓓ	11.	Ⓐ Ⓑ Ⓒ Ⓓ	17.	Ⓐ Ⓑ Ⓒ Ⓓ	23.	Ⓐ Ⓑ Ⓒ Ⓓ	29.	Ⓐ Ⓑ Ⓒ Ⓓ
6.	Ⓐ Ⓑ Ⓒ Ⓓ	12.	Ⓐ Ⓑ Ⓒ Ⓓ	18.	Ⓐ Ⓑ Ⓒ Ⓓ	24.	Ⓐ Ⓑ Ⓒ Ⓓ	30.	Ⓐ Ⓑ Ⓒ Ⓓ

PROBABILITY

LEARNING OBJECTIVES

➤ Basic concepts of Probability

MULTIPLE CHOICE QUESTIONS

1. There are 25 cards numbered from 1 to 25. One card is drawn at random. What is the probability that the number on this card is not divisible by 4?

   (A) $\dfrac{19}{25}$ (B) $\dfrac{6}{25}$

   (C) $\dfrac{21}{25}$ (D) $\dfrac{4}{25}$

2. Two dice are thrown simultaneously. What is the probability of getting 9 as the sum of two numbers that turn up?

   (A) $\dfrac{5}{36}$ (B) $\dfrac{1}{9}$

   (C) $\dfrac{1}{12}$ (D) $\dfrac{1}{6}$

3. A bag contains tickets marked with numbers 179, 180, 172, 127, 115, 115, 122, 143, 175, 222, 232, 162, 112, 132, 192, 182, 174, 132, 132, 131. A ticket is drawn at random. Find the probability that the ticket drawn has an even digit at 10's place.

   (A) $\dfrac{7}{19}$ (B) $\dfrac{3}{20}$

   (C) $\dfrac{7}{20}$ (D) $\dfrac{6}{19}$

4. A man calculates that the probability of his winning the first prize in a lottery is 0.08. If 6000 tickets are sold, how many tickets has he bought?

   (A) 480
   (B) 720
   (C) 240
   (D) 140

5. A lot of 24 bulbs contains 25% defective bulbs. A bulb is drawn at random from the lot. It is found to be not defective and it is not put back. Now one bulb is drawn at random from the rest. What is the probability that this bulb is not defective?

   (A) $\dfrac{15}{24}$ (B) $\dfrac{17}{23}$

   (C) $\dfrac{20}{23}$ (D) $\dfrac{18}{23}$

6. A die is thrown 350 times and the score of 6 obtained 28 times. Find the probability of getting a score under 6.

   (A) $\dfrac{2}{25}$ (B) $\dfrac{23}{25}$

   (C) $\dfrac{21}{25}$ (D) $\dfrac{1}{25}$

7. A box contains 5 red marbles, 7 black marbles and 3 white marbles. One marble is taken out from the box at random what is the probability that the marble taken out will be black or white?

OLYMPIAD WORKBOOK (IMO) CLASS – 10

(A) $\dfrac{2}{3}$ (B) $\dfrac{1}{3}$

(C) $\dfrac{4}{5}$ (D) None of these

8. What is the probability that a number selected at random from the numbers 1, 2, ... 35 is not a multiple of 7?

(A) $\dfrac{6}{7}$ (B) $\dfrac{5}{7}$

(C) $\dfrac{4}{7}$ (D) $\dfrac{3}{7}$

9. A bag contains 6 red balls, 8 white balls, 5 green balls and 3 black balls. One ball is drawn at random from the bag. Find the probability that the ball drawn is not white.

(A) $\dfrac{7}{11}$ (B) $\dfrac{8}{11}$

(C) $\dfrac{4}{11}$ (D) $\dfrac{9}{22}$

10. In a class, there are 35 boys and 15 girls. What is the probability of a randomly selected student of the class to be a girl?

(A) $\dfrac{3}{10}$ (B) $\dfrac{1}{5}$

(C) $\dfrac{2}{5}$ (D) None of these

11. Find the probability of getting 52 sunday in a leap year.

(A) $\dfrac{1}{7}$ (B) $\dfrac{5}{7}$

(C) $\dfrac{2}{7}$ (D) $\dfrac{3}{7}$

12. A box contains 6 green balls, 4 red balls and some white balls. If the probability of not drawing a white ball in one draw is $\dfrac{2}{3}$, what is the number of white balls?

(A) 5   (B) 6
(C) 7   (D) 4

13. A bag contains 5 red balls and some black balls. If the probability of drawing a black ball from the bag is twice that of a red ball find the number of black balls in the bag.

(A) 7   (B) 12
(C) 10   (D) 15

14. In a pack of 52 playing cards, the king, the queen, the jack and 10 are lost, all these cards are of spade. A card is drawn from the remaining well shuffled pack. Find the probability of getting a king.

(A) $\dfrac{3}{16}$ (B) $\dfrac{1}{16}$

(C) $\dfrac{1}{8}$ (D) $\dfrac{1}{12}$

15. A card is drawn from a well shuffled pack of 52 cards. Find the probability that the card drawn is a non ace.

(A) $\dfrac{12}{13}$ (B) $\dfrac{4}{13}$

(C) $\dfrac{2}{13}$ (D) $\dfrac{1}{13}$

16. A jar contains 54 marbles each of which is blue, green or white. The probability of getting a blue marble at random from the jar is $\dfrac{1}{3}$ and the probability of getting a green marble at random is $\dfrac{4}{9}$. What is the number of white marbles?

(A) 12
(B) 10
(C) 21
(D) 15

17. A number n is selected from the numbers 1, 2, 3 then a second number r is randomly selected from the numbers 2, 5, 7. What is probability that a product of nr of the two numbers will be less than 15?

(A) $\dfrac{7}{9}$ (B) $\dfrac{5}{9}$

(C) $\dfrac{1}{3}$ (D) $\dfrac{4}{9}$

18. In a bag there are seventy ₹1 coin, thirty ₹2 coin and fifty ₹5 coin. One coin is drawn at random. What is the probability that it will not be a ₹5 coin?

(A) $\dfrac{1}{3}$
(B) $\dfrac{2}{3}$
(C) $\dfrac{7}{15}$
(D) $\dfrac{1}{5}$

19. If a number x is chosen at random from the numbers −3, −2, −1, 1, 2, 3, 4 what is the probability that $x^2 < 12$?

(A) $\dfrac{6}{7}$
(B) $\dfrac{4}{7}$
(C) $\dfrac{3}{7}$
(D) $\dfrac{2}{7}$

20. A letter is chosen at random from the letters of word COMMUNICATION. What is the probability that the chosen letter is a vowel?

(A) $\dfrac{5}{13}$
(B) $\dfrac{7}{13}$
(C) $\dfrac{6}{13}$
(D) $\dfrac{4}{13}$

21. A bag contains 7 red balls, 8 green balls, 4 white balls and 5 black balls. If one ball is drawn at random what is the probability that the ball drawn is not green?

(A) $\dfrac{9}{24}$
(B) $\dfrac{1}{3}$
(C) $\dfrac{2}{3}$
(D) None of these

22. A letter is chosen at random from the letters of word CONCENTRATION. What is the probability that the chosen letter is a consonant?

(A) $\dfrac{8}{13}$
(B) $\dfrac{6}{13}$
(C) $\dfrac{5}{13}$
(D) $\dfrac{7}{13}$

23. Pravin and Navin are friends. What is the probability that both will have the same birthday, if the year was not a leap year?

(A) $\dfrac{1}{365}$
(B) $\dfrac{2}{365}$
(C) $\dfrac{364}{365}$
(D) None of these

24. 500 tickets of a lottery were sold. There are 15 prizes on these tickets. If Mohan has purchased one ticket, what is the probability that he will win a price?

(A) 0.03
(B) 0.01
(C) 0.05
(D) 0.04

25. There are 600 shirts in a carton in which 12 shirts are defective. One shirt is drawn at random. What is the probability that it is non-defective shirt?

(A) 0.98
(B) 0.96
(C) 0.02
(D) 0.04

26. The probability of a leap year selected at random containing 53 Sunday is:

 (A) $\dfrac{53}{366}$

 (B) $\dfrac{1}{7}$

 (C) $\dfrac{2}{7}$

 (D) $\dfrac{53}{365}$

27. A bag contains 3 red and 2 blue marbles. A marble is drawn at random. The probability of drawing a black ball is :

 (A) $\dfrac{3}{5}$

 (B) $\dfrac{2}{5}$

 (C) $\dfrac{0}{5}$

 (D) $\dfrac{1}{5}$

28. The probability that it will rain tomorrow is 0.85. What is the probability that it will not rain tomorrow

 (A) 0.25

 (B) 0.145

 (C) $\dfrac{3}{20}$

 (D) none of these

29. What is the probability that a number selected from the numbers (1, 2, 3,..........,15) is a multiple of 4?

 (A) $\dfrac{1}{5}$

 (B) $\dfrac{4}{5}$

 (C) $\dfrac{2}{15}$

 (D) $\dfrac{1}{3}$

30. What are the total outcomes when we throw three coins?

 (A) 4

 (B) 5

 (C) 8

 (D) 7

—Darken Your Choice with HB Pencil —

1.	Ⓐ	Ⓑ	Ⓒ	Ⓓ	7.	Ⓐ	Ⓑ	Ⓒ	Ⓓ	13.	Ⓐ Ⓑ Ⓒ Ⓓ				19	Ⓐ Ⓑ Ⓒ Ⓓ			25. Ⓐ Ⓑ Ⓒ Ⓓ
2.	Ⓐ	Ⓑ	Ⓒ	Ⓓ	8.	Ⓐ	Ⓑ	Ⓒ	Ⓓ	14.	Ⓐ Ⓑ Ⓒ Ⓓ				20.	Ⓐ Ⓑ Ⓒ Ⓓ			26. Ⓐ Ⓑ Ⓒ Ⓓ
3.	Ⓐ	Ⓑ	Ⓒ	Ⓓ	9.	Ⓐ	Ⓑ	Ⓒ	Ⓓ	15.	Ⓐ Ⓑ Ⓒ Ⓓ				21.	Ⓐ Ⓑ Ⓒ Ⓓ			27. Ⓐ Ⓑ Ⓒ Ⓓ
4.	Ⓐ	Ⓑ	Ⓒ	Ⓓ	10.	Ⓐ	Ⓑ	Ⓒ	Ⓓ	16.	Ⓐ Ⓑ Ⓒ Ⓓ				22.	Ⓐ Ⓑ Ⓒ Ⓓ			28. Ⓐ Ⓑ Ⓒ Ⓓ
5.	Ⓐ	Ⓑ	Ⓒ	Ⓓ	11.	Ⓐ	Ⓑ	Ⓒ	Ⓓ	17.	Ⓐ Ⓑ Ⓒ Ⓓ				23.	Ⓐ Ⓑ Ⓒ Ⓓ			29. Ⓐ Ⓑ Ⓒ Ⓓ
6.	Ⓐ	Ⓑ	Ⓒ	Ⓓ	12.	Ⓐ	Ⓑ	Ⓒ	Ⓓ	18.	Ⓐ Ⓑ Ⓒ Ⓓ				24.	Ⓐ Ⓑ Ⓒ Ⓓ			30. Ⓐ Ⓑ Ⓒ Ⓓ

LOGICAL REASONING

LEARNING OBJECTIVES

- ➤ Types of Analogy
- ➤ Types of Classification
- ➤ Basics of Coding
- ➤ Number test
- ➤ Solving questions related to Direction sense test
- ➤ Letter word problems
- ➤ Different types of Blood Relations
- ➤ Different types of mathematical operations
- ➤ Solving questions related to Series
- ➤ Solving questions related to Paper folding
- ➤ Solving questions related to Paper cutting
- ➤ Mirror images of letters

MULTIPLE CHOICE QUESTIONS

1. What number should replace the question mark?
   2836 : 13; 9423 : 14; 7229 : ?
   (A) 20   (B) 18
   (C) 16   (D) 12

2. 211 : 333 :: 356 : ?
   (A) 358   (B) 388
   (C) 423   (D) 459

3. TSR : FED :: WVU : ?
   (A) MLK
   (B) GFH
   (C) CAB
   (D) PQS

4. (A) Snake   (B) Whale
   (C) Lizard   (D) Crocodile

5. (A) Bangle   (B) Necklace
   (C) Ring   (D) Ornament

6. (A) Canada   (B) Europe
   (C) Australia   (D) Asia

7. If COME is coded as BNLD, then BRING will be coded as
   (A) BSHMF
   (B) BPJMH
   (C) AQHMF
   (D) APJMH

8. In a certain code if SILVER is REVLIS then BLACK will be coded as
   (A) KCALB   (B) KACBL
   (C) KCLAB   (D) KCBAL

9. In a certain code 3456 is coded as ROPE, 15526 is coded as APPLE. then 54613 will be coded as–
   (A) PEORA   (B) RPOEA
   (C) PROEA   (D) POEAR

10. If the seventh day of a month is three days earlier than Friday, what day will be on the nineteenth day of the month?
    (A) Friday   (B) Sunday
    (C) Monday   (D) Wednesday

11. In a queue *P* is eighteenth from the front while *Q* is sixteenth from the back. If *R* is twenty fifth from the front and is exactly in the middle position of *P* and *Q* then how many people are there in queue?
    (A) 47
    (B) 46
    (C) 45
    (D) 48

12. If 3 is subtracted from the middle digit of each of the following numbers and then the positions of the digits are reversed. Which of the following will be the last digit of the middle number after they are arranged in descending order
    589, 362, 554, 371, 442
    (A) 1
    (B) 2
    (C) 3
    (D) 4

13. John leaves his house and walks 12 km towards North. He turns right and walks another 12 km. He turns right again walks 12 km more and turns left to walk 5 km. How far is he from his home and in which direction?
    (A) 7 km, East
    (B) 24 km, East
    (C) 10 km, East
    (D) 17 km, East

14. *A*, *B*, *C*, *D*, *E*, *F*, *G*, and *H* are sitting around a round table in the same order for group discussion at equal distance. Their positions are clockwise. If *G* sits in the north then what will be the position of *D*.
    (A) South–East
    (B) South
    (C) South–West
    (D) East

15. Dinesh starts walking straight towards East. After walking 75 meters, he turns to the left and walks 25 meters straight. Again he turns to the left walks a distance of 40 meters straight, again he turns to the left and walks a distance of 25 meters. How far is he from the starting point?
    (A) 50 meters
    (B) 25 meteres
    (C) 35 meters
    (D) 115 meters

16. UNCONSCIOUS
    (A) NOSE
    (B) COIN
    (C) SUN
    (D) SON

17. CONTEMPORARY
    (A) PARROT
    (B) PRAYER
    (C) COMPANY
    (D) CARPENTER

18. REFRIGERATE
    (A) REFER
    (B) REGENERATE
    (C) RAGE
    (D) GATE

19. Soni who is Mishra's daughter, says to Punam "your mother Mamta is the youngest sister of my father. Mishra's father's child is Prabhat". How is Prabhat related to Punam?
    (A) Father
    (B) Uncle
    (C) Father in law
    (D) Grandmother

20. Pointing towards a man in the photograph Rekha said, "He is the son of only son of my grandmother." How is the man related to Rekha?
    (A) Cousin
    (B) Son
    (C) Nephew
    (D) Brother

21. Ramesh told Suresh, "Yesterday I defeated the only brother of the daughter of my grandmother". Whom did Ramesh defeat?
    (A) Father
    (B) Son
    (C) Brother
    (D) Father in law

22. If $20 - 10$ means 200, $8 \div 4$ means 12, 6×2 means 4, then $100 - 10 \times 1000 \div 1000 + 100 \times 10 = ?$
    (A) 20
    (B) 1000
    (C) 0
    (D) 1900

23. If *A* stands for +, *B* stands for −, *C* stands for × then what is the value of $(10\,C\,4)\,A\,(4\,C\,4)\,B\,6$?
    (A) 56
    (B) 46
    (C) 60
    (D) 50

24. If + means −, − means ×, ÷ means + and × means ÷ then $(3 - 15 \div 19) \times 8 + 6 = ?$
    (A) 2
    (B) 4
    (C) 8
    (D) −1

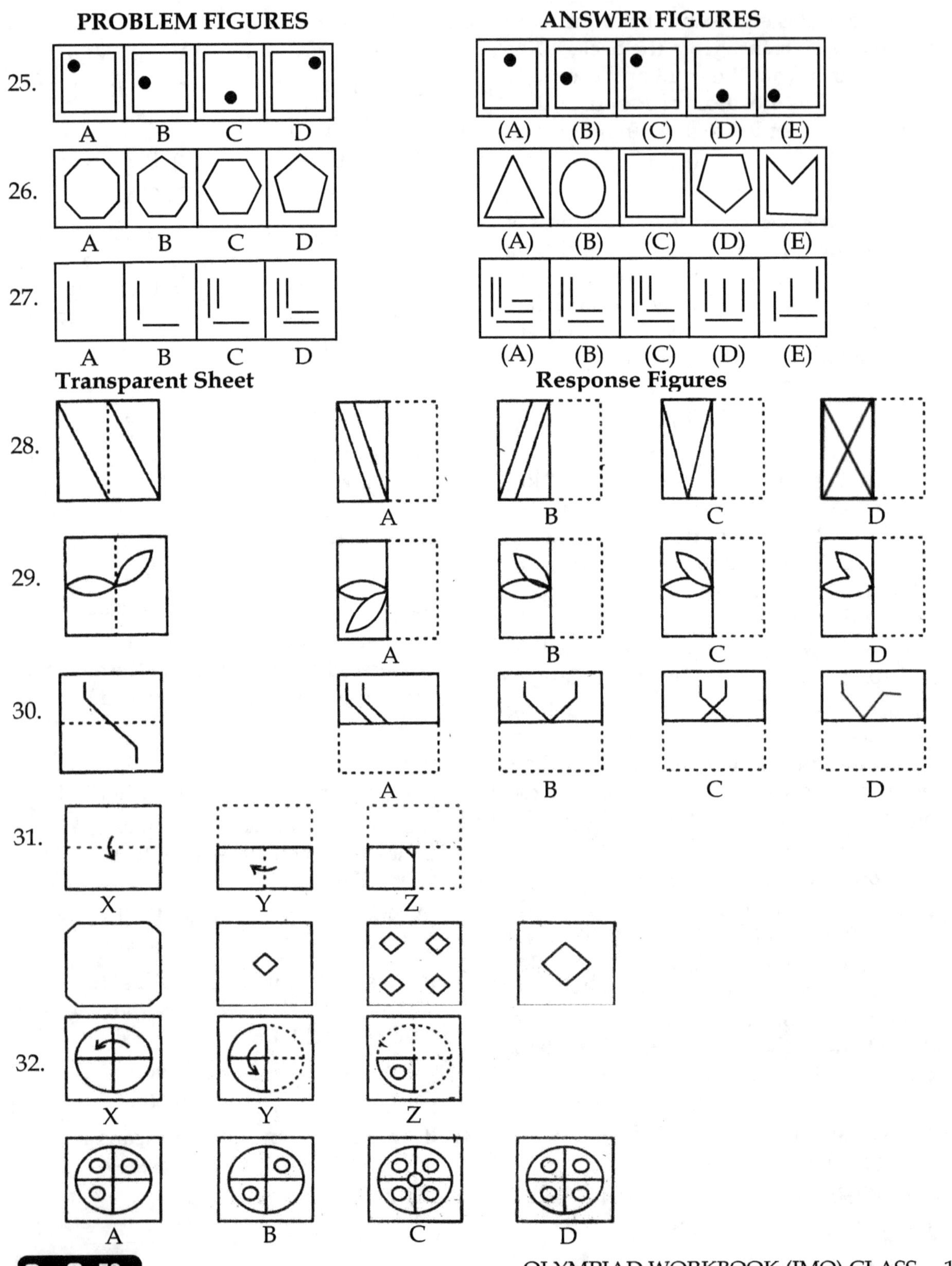

OLYMPIAD WORKBOOK (IMO) CLASS — 10

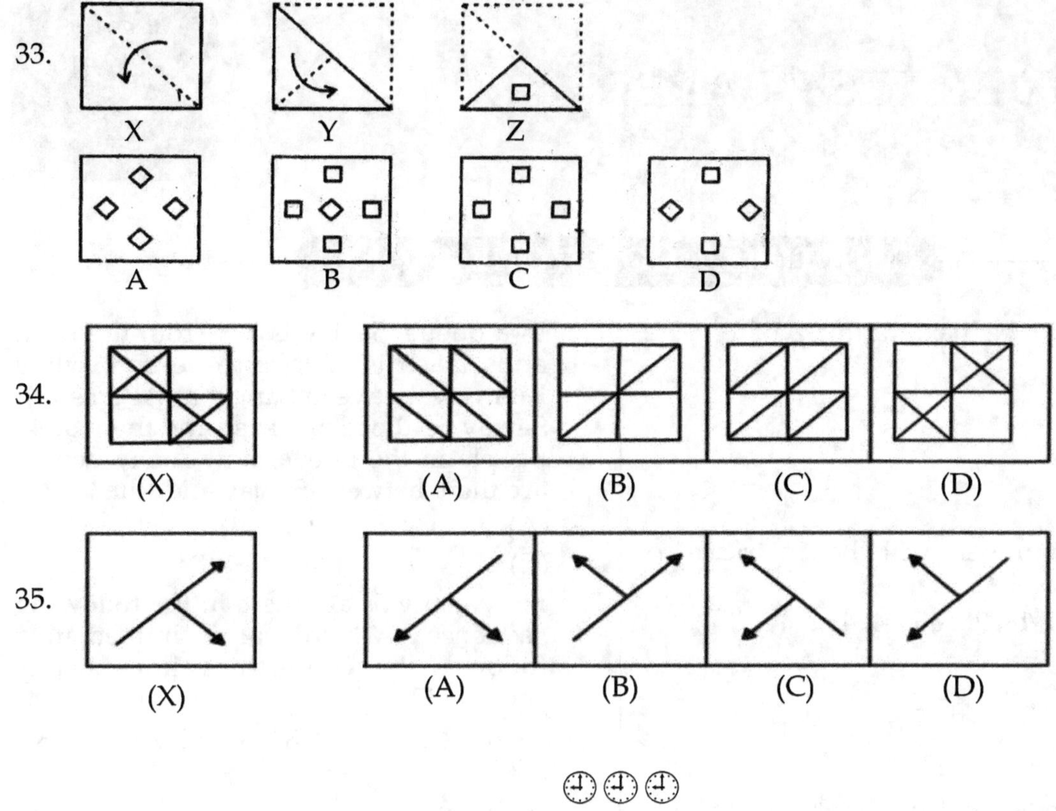

33.

34.

35.

1.	Ⓐ Ⓑ Ⓒ Ⓓ	8.	Ⓐ Ⓑ Ⓒ Ⓓ	15.	Ⓐ Ⓑ Ⓒ Ⓓ	22	Ⓐ Ⓑ Ⓒ Ⓓ	29.	Ⓐ Ⓑ Ⓒ Ⓓ
2.	Ⓐ Ⓑ Ⓒ Ⓓ	9.	Ⓐ Ⓑ Ⓒ Ⓓ	16.	Ⓐ Ⓑ Ⓒ Ⓓ	23.	Ⓐ Ⓑ Ⓒ Ⓓ	30.	Ⓐ Ⓑ Ⓒ Ⓓ
3.	Ⓐ Ⓑ Ⓒ Ⓓ	10.	Ⓐ Ⓑ Ⓒ Ⓓ	17.	Ⓐ Ⓑ Ⓒ Ⓓ	24.	Ⓐ Ⓑ Ⓒ Ⓓ	31.	Ⓐ Ⓑ Ⓒ Ⓓ
4.	Ⓐ Ⓑ Ⓒ Ⓓ	11.	Ⓐ Ⓑ Ⓒ Ⓓ	18.	Ⓐ Ⓑ Ⓒ Ⓓ	25.	Ⓐ Ⓑ Ⓒ Ⓓ	32.	Ⓐ Ⓑ Ⓒ Ⓓ
5.	Ⓐ Ⓑ Ⓒ Ⓓ	12.	Ⓐ Ⓑ Ⓒ Ⓓ	19.	Ⓐ Ⓑ Ⓒ Ⓓ	26.	Ⓐ Ⓑ Ⓒ Ⓓ	33.	Ⓐ Ⓑ Ⓒ Ⓓ
6.	Ⓐ Ⓑ Ⓒ Ⓓ	13.	Ⓐ Ⓑ Ⓒ Ⓓ	20.	Ⓐ Ⓑ Ⓒ Ⓓ	27.	Ⓐ Ⓑ Ⓒ Ⓓ	34.	Ⓐ Ⓑ Ⓒ Ⓓ
7.	Ⓐ Ⓑ Ⓒ Ⓓ	14.	Ⓐ Ⓑ Ⓒ Ⓓ	21.	Ⓐ Ⓑ Ⓒ Ⓓ	28.	Ⓐ Ⓑ Ⓒ Ⓓ	35.	Ⓐ Ⓑ Ⓒ Ⓓ

LOGICAL REASONING

MODEL TEST PAPER

1. What will be next term in BDF, CFL, DHL?
   (A) CJM
   (B) EJO
   (C) EMI
   (D) EIM

2. Which number will be in place of question mark?

   1, 5, 7, 14, 18, 20, 40, 44, 46,?
   (A) 48
   (B) 52
   (C) 92
   (D) 50

3. Which letter will be the 8th to the right of the 3rd letter of the second half of the English alphabet?
   (A) X
   (B) Y
   (C) W
   (D) V

4. Which one word cannot be made from the letters of the word COINCIDES?
   (A) COIN
   (B) NOSE
   (C) SUN
   (D) SON

5. In a certain code RADIO is XZOPL, SHEET is NBGGI, then what is the code for HEATER?
   (A) BGZIGX
   (B) BNGZIX
   (C) BGZGIK
   (D) GZBIXZ

6. In a queue, Sanjay is 14th from the front and Akash is 17th from the end, while Rita is in between Sanjay and Akash. If Sanjay be ahead of Akash and there be 48 people in the queue, how many people are there between Sanjay and Rita?
   (A) 5 (B) 6
   (C) 7 (D) 8

7. How many 5s are there in the following sequence which are immediately followed by 3 but not immediately preceded by 7?

   8 9 5 3 2 5 3 8 5 5 6 8 7 3 3 5 7 7 5 3 6 5 3 3 5 7 3 8
   (A) One
   (B) Two
   (C) Three
   (D) Four

8. Ram introduces Mohit as the son of the only brother of his father's wife. How is Mohit related to Ram?
   (A) Son
   (B) Cousin
   (C) Son-in-law
   (D) Uncle

9. If '+' means 'divided by', '–' means added, '×' means subtracted from, and ÷ means 'multiplied by' then what is the value of $24 \div 12 - 18 + 9 = ?$
   (A) 0.72
   (B) 290
   (C) –25
   (D) 15.30

10. Rajesh leaves for his office from his house. He walks towards East. After moving a distance of 20 m, he turns South and walks 10 m. Then he walks 35 m towards the West and further 5 m towards North. He then turns towards East and walks 15 m. What is the straight distance between his initial and final position?

(A) 5m

(B) 10m

(C) 15m

(D) 0m

11. It was Saturday, on January 12, 1980. The day of the week on January 12, 1979 is

(A) Sunday

(B) Friday

(C) Saturday

(D) Thursday

12. What is the number in the question mark?

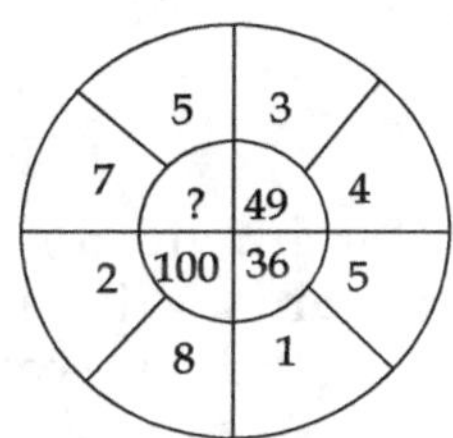

(A) 75   (B) 144

(C) 72   (D) None of these

13. Supervisor : Worker : : ?

(A) Junior : Senior

(B) Officer : Clerk

(C) Elder : Younger

(D) Debtor : Creditor

14. Select the lettered pair, that has the same relationship as the original pair of words

Sneer : Contempt

(A) Snarl : Restlessness

(B) Grimace : Pain

(C) Joke : Happiness

(D) Mourn : Frustration

15. Choose the most appropriate description about these three words

Naive : Gulleless : Ingenue

(A) The terms are used for criminals

(B) These terms are connected with bad society manners.

(C) They depict various shades of innocence

(D) These are words used by social workers

16. Choose the number which has the same relationship with the 3rd number as first two numbers are related?

583 : 293 : : 753 : ?

(A) 378   (B) 487

(C) 291   (D) 581

17. Choose the odd pair/group.

(A) 22, 45   (B) 31, 48

(C) 37, 49   (D) 54, 13

18. In a certain code MOTHER is written as ONHURF. How will ANSWER be written in that code?

(A) NBXSSE

(B) NBWRRF

(C) MAVSPE

(D) NBWTRF

19. If MINJUR is coded as 312547 and TADA as 6898. In that code, how can MADURAI be coded?

(A) 3894781   (B) 3894871

(C) 3498178   (D) 3849781

20. Two ladies and two men are playing cards and are seated at North, East, South and West of a table. No lady is facing East. People seating opposite to each other are not of the same sex. One man is facing South. Which directions are the ladies facing?

(A) East and West

(B) North and East

(C) South and East

(D) North and Wes

21. For what value of k will the equation $2x + 2y + 7 = 0$, $4x + ky + 14 = 0$ represents coincident lines?

(A) 3   (B) 4

(C) 5   (D) –4

22. If E is a point on side AC of equilateral triangle ABC such that $BE \perp AC$ then what is the value of $AB^2 + BC^2 + AC^2$?

(A) $2BE^2$ (B) $3BE^2$

(C) $6BE^2$ (D) $4BE^2$

23. If $\tan\theta = \dfrac{1}{\sqrt{3}}$ then what is the value of

$$\frac{\cosec^2\theta - \sec^2\theta}{\cosec^2\theta + \sec^2\theta}?$$

(A) $-\dfrac{1}{2}$ (B) $\dfrac{1}{2}$

(C) –1   (D) –1

24. Find the ratio in which the x-axis divides the line segment joining the point $(12, -3)$ and $(3, 6)$.

(A) 1:2   (B) 2:1

(C) 1:–2   (D) –2:1

25. An arc of a circle is of length 5π cm and the sector it bounds has an area of 20π cm^2. What is the radius of the circle?

(A) 8 cm   (B) 4 cm

(C) 12 cm   (D) 16 cm

26. Which of the following rational numbers have terminating decimal?

(A) $\dfrac{7}{250}$ (B) $\dfrac{2}{21}$

(C) $\dfrac{16}{225}$ (D) $\dfrac{5}{76}$

27. If the centroid of the triangle formed by the point (a, b), (b, c) and (c, a) is at the origin. then $a^3 + b^3 + c^3 = ?$

(A) abc

(B) $a + b + c$

(C) $3\,abc$

(D) 0

28. The area of a circle whose area and circumference are numerically equal is

(A) 2π sq. units   (B) 8π sq. units

(C) 4π sq. units   (D) 5π sq. units

29. The 9th term of an A.P. is 449 and 449th term is 9. Which term of this A.P. is zero?

(A) 502th   (B) 458th

(C) 497st   (D) 503th

30. Find the quadratic equation whose one root is 2 and the sum of whose roots is zero.

(A) $x^2 - 4 = 0$

(B) $x^2 + 4 = 0$

(C) $x^2 - 2 = 0$

(D) $4x^2 - 1 = 0$

31. If the mean of first n natural number is $\dfrac{5n}{9}$, then what is the value of n?

(A) 8   (B) 9

(C) 4   (D) 10

32. What is the value of $9\sec^2\theta - 9\tan^2\theta$?

(A) 8   (B) 9

(C) 0   (D) 1

33. One card is drawn from a well shuffled pack of 52 cards. What is the probability of getting a black face card?

(A) $\dfrac{3}{26}$ (B) $\dfrac{3}{14}$

(C) $\dfrac{3}{13}$ (D) $\dfrac{1}{26}$

34. The ratio between the radius of the base and the height of the cylinder is 2:3. If its volume is 1617 cm^3, what is the total surface area of the cylinder?

(A) 462 cm^2

(B) 770 cm^2

(C) 540 cm^2

(D) 308 cm^2

35. A sector of 56°, cut out from a circle, contain 17.6 cm^2. What is radius of that circle?

(A) 4 cm   (B) 5 cm

(C) 6 cm   (D) 8 cm

36. On decreasing the radius of the circle by 30%, its area is decreased by what percent?
   (A) 45% (B) 51%
   (C) 60% (D) 30%

37. The points P (0, –2), Q (3, 1), R (0, 4) and S (–3, 1) are vertices of a
   (A) Square
   (B) Rhombus
   (C) Parallelogram
   (D) Rectangle

38. If the $\sin 3\theta = \cos(\theta - 6°)$ where 3θ and $(\theta - 6)$ are acute angles, then what is the value of θ?
   (A) 36° (B) 66°
   (C) 24° (D) 54°

39. For what values of k, the system of equations $2x + 3y = 7$, $(k - 1) x + (k + 2) y = 3k$ has an infinite number of solutions?
   (A) $k = 3$ (B) $k = 7$
   (C) $k = 4$ (D) $k = 5$

40. Which term of A.P 24, 21, 18,15 .... is the first negative term?
   (A) 10ᵗʰ (B) 12ᵗʰ
   (C) 9ᵗʰ (D) 8ᵗʰ

41. A rectangular field is 20 m long and 14 m width. There is a path of equal width all around it having an area of 111 m². Find the width of the path.
   (A) 1.5 m
   (B) 2.5 m
   (C) 2 m
   (D) 3 m

42. If α, β, γ be the zeros of the polynomial $f(x)$ such that $\alpha + \beta + \gamma = 3$, $\alpha\beta + \beta\gamma + r\alpha = -10$ and $\alpha\beta\gamma = -24$ then what is the polynomial $f(x)$
   (A) $x^3 + 3x^2 - 10x + 24$
   (B) $x^3 + 6x^2 + 10x - 24$
   (C) $x^3 - 3x^2 - 10x + 24$
   (D) $x^3 + 3x^2 + 10x - 24$

43. $1.23\,\overline{48}$ is
   (A) a rational number
   (B) an integer
   (C) an irrational number
   (D) None of these

44. If 35 is removed from the data 30, 34, 35, 36, 37, 38, 39, 40, then the median is increased by
   (A) 2.5
   (B) 1.5
   (C) 0.5
   (D) 3.5

45. If one root of the equation $x^2 + ax + 3 = 0$ is one, then the other root is
   (A) –3 (B) 2
   (C) –2 (D) 3

46. If the angles of elevation of the top of a tower from two points distant a and b from the base and in the same straight line with it are complementary, what is the height of the tower?
   (A) ab

   (B) $\dfrac{a}{b}$

   (C) $\sqrt{\dfrac{a}{b}}$

   (D) $\sqrt{ab}$

47. Let S_1, S_2, S_3 be the sum of n, $2n$, $3n$ forms of an A.P respectively then which of the following alternative is correct?
   (A) $S_3 = 3S_2 - 3S_1$
   (B) $S_2 = 2S_3 - 2S_1$
   (C) $S_3 = 3S_1 - 3S_2$
   (D) None of these

48. If $x = 1$ is a common root of $ax^2 + ax + 2 = 0$ and $x^2 + x + b = 0$ then what is the value of ab?
   (A) 1 (B) 3
   (C) 2 (D) 4

49. The radii of the circular ends of frustum are 6 cm and 14 cm. If its slant height is 10 cm then what is its vertical height?

(A) 7 cm

(B) 4 cm

(C) 8 cm

(D) 6 cm

50. It is given that $AP = PB$ then which of the following is correct?

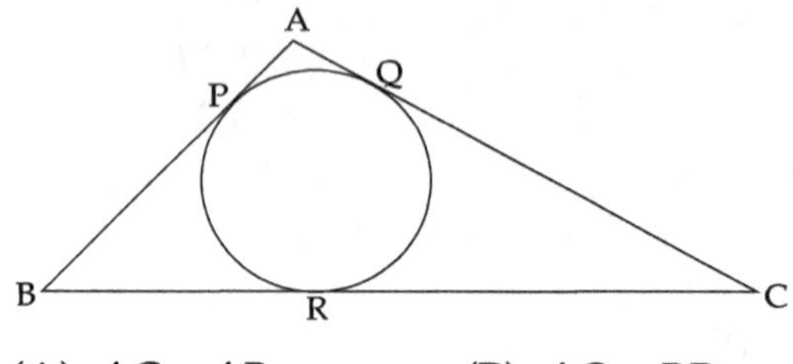

(A) $AC = AB$ (B) $AQ = BR$

(C) $AQ = QC$ (D) $AB = BC$

-Darken Your Choice with HB Pencil-

1.	Ⓐ Ⓑ Ⓒ Ⓓ	11.	Ⓐ Ⓑ Ⓒ Ⓓ	21.	Ⓐ Ⓑ Ⓒ Ⓓ	31.	Ⓐ Ⓑ Ⓒ Ⓓ	41.	Ⓐ Ⓑ Ⓒ Ⓓ
2.	Ⓐ Ⓑ Ⓒ Ⓓ	12.	Ⓐ Ⓑ Ⓒ Ⓓ	22.	Ⓐ Ⓑ Ⓒ Ⓓ	32.	Ⓐ Ⓑ Ⓒ Ⓓ	42.	Ⓐ Ⓑ Ⓒ Ⓓ
3.	Ⓐ Ⓑ Ⓒ Ⓓ	13.	Ⓐ Ⓑ Ⓒ Ⓓ	23.	Ⓐ Ⓑ Ⓒ Ⓓ	33.	Ⓐ Ⓑ Ⓒ Ⓓ	43.	Ⓐ Ⓑ Ⓒ Ⓓ
4.	Ⓐ Ⓑ Ⓒ Ⓓ	14.	Ⓐ Ⓑ Ⓒ Ⓓ	24.	Ⓐ Ⓑ Ⓒ Ⓓ	34.	Ⓐ Ⓑ Ⓒ Ⓓ	44.	Ⓐ Ⓑ Ⓒ Ⓓ
5.	Ⓐ Ⓑ Ⓒ Ⓓ	15.	Ⓐ Ⓑ Ⓒ Ⓓ	25.	Ⓐ Ⓑ Ⓒ Ⓓ	35.	Ⓐ Ⓑ Ⓒ Ⓓ	45.	Ⓐ Ⓑ Ⓒ Ⓓ
6.	Ⓐ Ⓑ Ⓒ Ⓓ	16.	Ⓐ Ⓑ Ⓒ Ⓓ	26.	Ⓐ Ⓑ Ⓒ Ⓓ	36.	Ⓐ Ⓑ Ⓒ Ⓓ	46.	Ⓐ Ⓑ Ⓒ Ⓓ
7.	Ⓐ Ⓑ Ⓒ Ⓓ	17.	Ⓐ Ⓑ Ⓒ Ⓓ	27.	Ⓐ Ⓑ Ⓒ Ⓓ	37.	Ⓐ Ⓑ Ⓒ Ⓓ	47.	Ⓐ Ⓑ Ⓒ Ⓓ
8.	Ⓐ Ⓑ Ⓒ Ⓓ	18.	Ⓐ Ⓑ Ⓒ Ⓓ	28.	Ⓐ Ⓑ Ⓒ Ⓓ	38.	Ⓐ Ⓑ Ⓒ Ⓓ	48.	Ⓐ Ⓑ Ⓒ Ⓓ
9.	Ⓐ Ⓑ Ⓒ Ⓓ	19.	Ⓐ Ⓑ Ⓒ Ⓓ	29.	Ⓐ Ⓑ Ⓒ Ⓓ	39.	Ⓐ Ⓑ Ⓒ Ⓓ	49.	Ⓐ Ⓑ Ⓒ Ⓓ
10.	Ⓐ Ⓑ Ⓒ Ⓓ	20.	Ⓐ Ⓑ Ⓒ Ⓓ	30.	Ⓐ Ⓑ Ⓒ Ⓓ	40.	Ⓐ Ⓑ Ⓒ Ⓓ	50.	Ⓐ Ⓑ Ⓒ Ⓓ

1. REAL NUMBERS

Answer Key

1. (A)	2. (C)	3. (A)	4. (B)	5. (B)	6. (A)	7. (C)	8. (C)	9. (B)	10. (D)
11. (C)	12. (B)	13. (B)	14. (B)	15. (C)	16. (A)	17. (B)	18. (A)	19. (B)	20. (A)
21. (D)	22. (B)	23. (B)	24. (C)	25. (A)					

1. (A)

$$\text{L.C.M.} = \frac{\text{product of numbers}}{\text{H.C.F. of numbers}}$$

$$= \frac{3072}{16} = 192$$

2. (C)

$398 - 7 = 391;\ 436 - 11 = 425;$

$542 - 15 = 527$

Required number = H.C.F. of 391, 425 and 527

$= 17$

3. (A)

$$\text{Other number} = \frac{\text{H.C.F.} \times \text{L.C.M.}}{\text{one number}}$$

$$= \frac{145 \times 2175}{725} = 435$$

4. (B)

L.C.M. of 35, 56, 91 = 3640

Remainder = 7

Required number = 3640 + 7 = 3647

8. (C)

We have $196 = 2^2 \times 7^2$

$2 + 2 = 4$

9. (B)

H.C.F. of 95 and 152 = 19

10. (D)

$\sqrt{27} \times \sqrt{3} = \sqrt{81} = 9$

12. (B)

$6^1 - 5^1 = 1$

$6^2 - 5^2 = 36 - 25 = 11$ and so on

13. (b)

$42 = 2 \times 3 \times 7$ and $63 = 3^2 \times 7$

LCM $= 2 \times 3^2 \times 7 = 126$

14. (B)

$576 = 2^6 \times 3^2$

$6 + 2 = 8$

15. (C)

Here $1225 = 5^2 \times 7^2$

$\therefore$ Required difference $= 2 - 2 = 0$

16. (A)

L.C.M. of 1, 2, 3, 4, 5, 6, 7, 8, 9, 10 = 2520

18. (A)

$13915 = 5 \times 11 \times 11 \times 23$

Required difference $= 23 - 5 = 18$

19. (B)

H.C.F. of 210 and 55 = 5

$210 \times 5 + 55y = 5$

$\Rightarrow \qquad 55y = 5 - 1050$

$\Rightarrow \qquad 55y = -1045$

$\Rightarrow \qquad y = \dfrac{-1045}{55} = -19$

20. (A)

$$\frac{43}{2^4 \times 5^3} = \frac{43}{16 \times 125}$$

21. (D)

Smallest prime number $= 2$

Smallest composite number $= 4$

$\therefore$ Required product $= 2 \times 4 = 8$

22. (B)

$\dfrac{21}{2^3 \times 5^6}$ as its denominator is in the form

$2^m \times 5^n$

23. (B)

Required product $=$ H.C.F. $\times$ L.C.M.

$= 1 \times 81 \times 50 = 4050$

25. (A)

L.C.M. $\times$ H.C.F. $= 306 \times 657$

$\Rightarrow$ L.C.M. $\times 9 = 306 \times 657$

$\Rightarrow$ L.C.M. $= \dfrac{306 \times 657}{9} = 22338$

HOTS (ACHIEVERS SECTION)

26. (D)	27. (B)	28. (B)	29. (B)	30. (C)

2. POLYNOMIALS

Answer Key

1. (B)	2. (A)	3. (A)	4. (A)	5. (D)	6. (A)	7. (C)	8. (A)	9. (B)	10. (A)
11. (A)	12. (B)	13. (A)	14. (B)	15. (D)	16. (B)	17. (A)	18. (D)	19. (A)	20. (A)
21. (A)	22. (B)	23. (B)	24. (B)	25. (A)					

1. (B)

Here

$$4x^2 + 3x - 2 \overline{)\, 8x^4 + 14x^3 - 2x^2 + 7x - 8\,}\, (2x^2 + 2x - 1$$

$$\underline{-8x^4 \pm 6x^3 \mp 4x^2}$$

$$8x^3 + 2x^2 + 7x$$

$$\underline{-8x^3 \pm 6x^2 \mp 4x}$$

$$-4x^2 + 11x - 8$$

$$\underline{\mp 4x^2 \mp 3x \pm 2}$$

$$14x - 10$$

$\therefore$ $14x - 10$ must be subtracted.

2. (A)

$2x^4 - 3x^3 - 3x^2 + 6x - 2$

Let the other roots be α and β.

Sum of the roots $= \sqrt{2} + (-\sqrt{2}) + \alpha + \beta = \dfrac{3}{2}$

$$\alpha + \beta = \dfrac{3}{2} \qquad \ldots(1)$$

Product of roots $= \dfrac{-2}{2} = -1$

$(\sqrt{2})(-\sqrt{2})\,\alpha\beta = -1 \Rightarrow \alpha\beta = \dfrac{1}{2} \qquad \ldots(2)$

$(\alpha - \beta)^2 = (\alpha + \beta)^2 - 4\alpha\beta$

$$= \left(\dfrac{3}{2}\right)^2 - 4\alpha\beta = \dfrac{9}{4} - \dfrac{4}{2} = \dfrac{1}{4}.$$

$$\alpha - \beta = \pm\dfrac{1}{2} \qquad \ldots(3)$$

From equation (1) and (3)

$\alpha = 1,\ \beta = \dfrac{1}{2}$ or $\beta = 1,\ \alpha = \dfrac{1}{2}$

3. (A)

Given $\alpha + \beta + \gamma = 2$

$\alpha\beta + \beta\gamma + \gamma\alpha = -7$

$\alpha\beta\gamma = -14$

Cubic polynomial is

$k(x^3 - 2x^2 - 7x + 14)$

4. (A)

Let the zeros be $\alpha,\ -\alpha,\ \beta$.

$\therefore$ $\alpha + (-\alpha) + \beta = -\left(\dfrac{-5}{1}\right) = 5$

$\Rightarrow \qquad \beta = 5$

and $(\alpha)(-\alpha)(\beta) = \dfrac{-80}{1}$

$\Rightarrow \qquad -\alpha^2\beta = -80 \Rightarrow \alpha^2\beta = 80$

$\Rightarrow \qquad \alpha^2 = \dfrac{80}{\beta} = \dfrac{80}{5} = 16$

$\Rightarrow \qquad \alpha = \pm 4$

The zeros are 4, –4, 5.

5. **(D)**

If α and β are two zeros then $\alpha\beta = 3$

Let third root be γ.

$\alpha\beta\gamma = \dfrac{-9}{2}$

$\Rightarrow \quad 3\gamma = \dfrac{-9}{2}$

$\Rightarrow \quad \gamma = -\dfrac{9}{2\times 3} = \dfrac{-3}{2}$

6. **(A)**

Given $\alpha + \beta + \gamma = 6$

$\alpha\beta + \beta\gamma + \gamma\alpha = -1$

$\alpha\beta\gamma = -30$

The cubic polynomial is

$P(x) = x^3 - (\alpha + \beta + \gamma)x^2 + (\alpha\beta + \beta\gamma + \gamma\alpha)x - \alpha\beta\gamma$

$= x^3 - 6x^2 - x - (-30)$

(substituting the given values)

$= x^3 - 6x^2 - x + 30$

7. **(C)**

The given polynomial is

$2x^3 + x^2 - 13x + 6$

$\alpha,\ \beta,\ \gamma$ are its zeros

$\therefore \quad \alpha\beta\gamma = \dfrac{-d}{a} = \dfrac{-6}{2} = -3$

8. **(A)**

Polynomial $= (-x^2 + x - 1)(x - 2) + 3$

$-x^3 + 2x^2 + x^2 - 2x - x + 2 + 3$

$= -x^3 + 3x^2 - 3x + 5$

9. **(B)**

Here

$$x^2 + 2x - 3 \overline{)4x^4 + 2x^3 - 2x^2 + x - 1}\ (4x^2 - 6x + 22$$
$$\underline{\pm 4x^4 \pm 8x^3 \mp 12x^2}$$
$$-6x^3 + 10x^2 + x$$
$$\underline{\mp 6x^3 \mp 12x^2 \pm 18x}$$
$$22x^2 - 17x - 1$$
$$\underline{\pm 22x^2 \pm 44x \mp 66}$$
$$-61x + 65$$

Clearly $-61x + 65$ must be added.

10. **(A)**

$$3x^2 + 4x + 1 \overline{)6x^4 + 8x^3 + 17x^2 + 21x + 7}\ (2x^2 + 5$$
$$\underline{\pm 6x^4 \pm 8x^3 \pm 2x^2}$$
$$15x^2 + 21x + 7$$
$$\underline{-15x^2 \pm 20x + 5}$$
$$x + 2$$

remainder $= x + 2$

$ax + b = x + 2$ (Given)

$\Rightarrow a = 1;\ b = 2$

11. **(A)**

Required polynomial

$= x^3 - (\alpha + \beta + \gamma)x^2 + (\alpha\beta + \beta\gamma + \gamma\alpha)x - \alpha\beta\gamma$

$= x^3 - 4x^2 + x + 6$

12. **(B)**

We have $\alpha + \beta + \gamma = -2 - 3 - 1 = -6$

$\alpha\beta + \beta\gamma + \gamma\alpha$

$\qquad = (-2)(-3) + (-3)(-1) + (-1)(-2)$

$\qquad = 6 + 3 + 2 = 11$

and $\quad \alpha\beta\gamma = (-2)(-3)(-1) = -6$

$\therefore$ Required polynomial

$\qquad = x^3 - (-6)x^2 + 11x - (-6)$

$\qquad = x^3 + 6x^2 + 11x + 6$

13. **(A)**

$x^2 - (\text{Sum of zeros})\,x + \text{Product of zeros}$

$x^2 - (-5)\,x + (-12) = x^2 + 5x - 12$

14. **(B)**

Here $(2 - x + x^2)(3x - 1)$

$= 6x - 2 - 3x^2 + x + 3x^3 - x^2$

$= 3x^3 - 4x^2 + 7x - 2$

15. **(D)**

We have $x^2 - 2x - 3$

$$\therefore \quad x = \frac{-(-2) \pm \sqrt{4+12}}{2}$$

$$= \frac{2 \pm 4}{2} = \frac{2+4}{2}, \frac{2-4}{2} = 3, -1$$

16. (B)

Here $\alpha + \beta = \dfrac{2}{3} - \dfrac{1}{4} = \dfrac{8-3}{12} = \dfrac{5}{12}$

$$\alpha\beta = \left(\frac{2}{3}\right)\left(-\frac{1}{4}\right) = -\frac{1}{6}$$

$\therefore$ Required polynomial $= x^2 - \dfrac{5}{12}x - \dfrac{1}{6}$

$$= \frac{12x^2 - 5x - 2}{12}$$

17. (A)

α, β are zeros of $2x^2 + 5x - 10$

then $\alpha\beta = \dfrac{-10}{2} = -5$

18. (D)

We have $x^3 + 4x^2 + x - 6$

Comparing above equation by

$x^3 - (\alpha + \beta + \gamma)x^2 + (\alpha\beta + \beta\gamma + \gamma\alpha)x - \alpha\beta\gamma$

$\Rightarrow \alpha\beta\gamma = 6$

19. (A)

Here $l + m + n = p$, $lmn = r$

Now $\dfrac{1}{lm} + \dfrac{1}{mn} + \dfrac{1}{nl} = \dfrac{n+l+m}{lmn} = \dfrac{p}{r}$

20. (A)

Let one zero be α

Then other zero $= \dfrac{1}{\alpha}$

$\therefore \quad \alpha + \dfrac{1}{\alpha} = \dfrac{-13}{K^2 + 4}$

$$\alpha \times \frac{1}{\alpha} = \frac{4K}{K^2 + 4}$$

$\Rightarrow K^2 + 4 = 4K$

$\Rightarrow K^2 - 4K + 4 = 0$

$\Rightarrow (K-2)^2 = 0$

$\Rightarrow K = 2$

21. (A)

Required polynomial

$= x^2 - (\alpha + \beta)x + \alpha\beta$

$\Rightarrow x^2 - (-6)x + (-4) = x^2 + 6x - 4$

22. (B)

The given polynomial is $4\sqrt{3}x^2 + 5x - 2\sqrt{3}$

$\therefore \quad \alpha\beta = \dfrac{-2\sqrt{3}}{4\sqrt{3}} = \dfrac{-1}{2}$

23. (B)

$$-x^2 + x - 1 \overline{)-x^3 + 3x^2 - 3x + 5} \, (x - 2$$

$$\underline{\mp x^3 \pm x^2 \mp x}$$

$$2x^2 - 2x + 5$$

$$\underline{\pm 2x^2 \mp 2x \pm 2}$$

$$3$$

24. (B)

$$3x^2 + 2x - 4 \overline{)30x^4 + 11x^3 - 82x^2 - 12x + 48} \, (10x^2 - 3x - 12$$

$$\underline{\pm 30x^4 \pm 20x^3 \mp 40x^2}$$

$$-9x^3 - 42x^2 - 12x$$

$$\underline{\mp 9x^3 \mp 6x^2 \pm 12x}$$

$$-36x^2 - 24x + 48$$

$$\underline{\mp 36x^2 \mp 24x \pm 48}$$

25. (A)

Given α and β are zeros of $x^2 - px + d$

then $\alpha + \beta = \dfrac{-(-p)}{1} = p$

and $\alpha\beta = \dfrac{d}{1} = d$

$\therefore \quad \dfrac{1}{\alpha} + \dfrac{1}{\beta} = \dfrac{\alpha + \beta}{\alpha\beta} = \dfrac{p}{d}$

HOTS (ACHIEVERS SECTION)

26. (D)	27. (C)	28. (D)	29. (D)	30. (B)

Answer Key

1. (C)	2. (A)	3. (B)	4. (B)	5. (B)	6. (A)	7. (A)	8. (B)	9. (A)	10. (D)
11. (C)	12. (C)	13. (B)	14. (B)	15. (C)	16. (A)	17. (A)	18. (C)	19. (A)	20. (A)
21. (A)	22. (A)	23. (B)	24. (A)	25. (B)					

1. (C)

For a non–zero solution,

$$\frac{a_1}{a_2} = \frac{b_1}{b_2} \Rightarrow \frac{3}{k} = \frac{5}{10} \Rightarrow k = \frac{10 \times 3}{5} = 6$$

2. (A)

For no solution, it must have

$$\frac{a_1}{a_2} = \frac{b_1}{b_2} \neq \frac{c_1}{c_2}$$

$$\frac{3}{2k-1} = \frac{1}{k-1} \neq \frac{-1}{-(2k+1)}$$

$$3k - 3 = 2k - 1 \Rightarrow k = 2$$

3. (B)

Let $\dfrac{1}{x} = m$, $\dfrac{1}{y} = n$

Then $am - bn = 0$ ...(1)

$ab^2m + a^2bn = a^2 + b^2$ ...(2)

Now $am - bn + 0 = 0$

$ab^2m + a^2bn - (a^2 + b^2) = 0$

By cross multiplication,

$$\frac{m}{b(a^2 + b^2)} = \frac{n}{a(a^2 + b^2)} = \frac{1}{(a^3b + ab^3)}$$

$$m = \frac{b(a^2 + b^2)}{ab(a^2 + b^2)} = \frac{1}{a} \Rightarrow \frac{1}{x} = \frac{1}{a} \Rightarrow x = a$$

$$n = \frac{a(a^2 + b^2)}{ab(a^2 + b^2)} = \frac{1}{b} \Rightarrow \frac{1}{y} = \frac{1}{b} \Rightarrow y = b$$

4. (B)

We have

$2ax - 2by = -a - 4b$ ...(1)

and $2bx + 2ay = 4a - b$ ...(2)

Now $2a^2x - 2aby = -a^2 - 4ab$ ...(3)

$2b^2x + 2aby = 4ab - b^2$ ...(4)

Adding (3) and (4) we get,

$$2x(a^2 + b^2) = -(a^2 + b^2) \Rightarrow x = \frac{-1}{2}$$

Putting $x = -\frac{1}{2}$ in eqn (2)

$$2b\left(\frac{-1}{2}\right) + 2ay = 4a - b$$

$$\Rightarrow -b + 2ay = 4a - b \Rightarrow 2ay = 4a$$

$$\Rightarrow y = \frac{4a}{2a} = 2$$

5. (B)

For infinitely many solutions,

$$\frac{a_1}{a_2} = \frac{b_1}{b_2} = \frac{c_1}{c_2}$$

$$\Rightarrow \frac{3}{m+n} = \frac{4}{2(m-n)} = \frac{-12}{1-5m}$$

On solving these equations, we get

$m = 5, n = +1$

6. (A)

Let the breadth of field be x m and length be y m.

Then, area $= xy$ m^2

Now $y = 3 + x$

$\Rightarrow y - x = 3$ ...(1)

New length $= y + 3$

breadth $= x - 2$

$\therefore$ area $= (x - 2)(y + 3) = xy$

$\Rightarrow xy + 3x - 2y - 6 = xy$

$\Rightarrow 3x - 2y = 6$ ...(2)

From (1) and (2), we get

$x = 12$ m, $y = 15$ m

7. (A)

Here

$$bx + by = ab + b^2 \qquad \text{...(1)}$$
$$\text{and} \quad ax - by = a^2 - b^2 \qquad \text{...(2)}$$

Adding, $x(a + b) = a(b + a) \Rightarrow x = a$

Putting $x = a$ in eqn (2), we have
$$a^2 - by = a^2 - b^2$$
$$\Rightarrow -by = -b^2 \Rightarrow y = b$$

Hence $\quad x = a, y = b$

8. **(B)**

Here
$$2x + 3y - 5 = 0$$
$$\text{and} \quad kx - 6y - 8 = 0$$

For a unique solution, $\dfrac{a_1}{a_2} \neq \dfrac{b_1}{b_2}$

$$\frac{2}{k} \neq \frac{3}{-6} \Rightarrow k \neq -4$$

9. **(A)**

Given
$$2x - ky + 3 = 0$$
$$3x + 2y - 1 = 0$$

For no solution, we have
$$\frac{a_1}{a_2} = \frac{b_1}{b_2} \neq \frac{c_1}{c_2}$$

$$\frac{a_1}{a_2} = \frac{2}{3}, \frac{b_1}{b_2} = \frac{-k}{2}, \frac{c_1}{c_2} = \frac{3}{-1}$$

Now $\quad \dfrac{a_1}{a_2} = \dfrac{2}{3} \neq \dfrac{c_1}{c_2} = \dfrac{3}{-1}$

So, $\dfrac{a_1}{a_2} = \dfrac{b_1}{b_2} \Rightarrow \dfrac{2}{3} = \dfrac{-k}{2} \Rightarrow k = \dfrac{-4}{3}$

10. **(A)**

Let Shashi's present age be x and Ravi's present age be y.
$$y - 5 = 3(x - 5) \Rightarrow 3x - y = 10 \qquad \text{...(1)}$$
$$y + 10 = 2(x + 10) \Rightarrow 2x - y = -10 \qquad \text{...(2)}$$

Solving eqns (1) and (2), we get
$$x = 20, y = 50$$

11. **(C)**

Let the fraction be $\dfrac{x}{y}$

then $\quad x + y = 12 \qquad \text{...(1)}$

and $\qquad \dfrac{x}{y + 3} = \dfrac{1}{2} \Rightarrow 2x - y = 3 \qquad \text{...(2)}$

By solving eqn (1) and (2), we get $x = 5, y = 7$

$$\frac{x}{y} = \frac{5}{7}$$

12. **(C)**

In a cyclic quadrilateral,
$$\angle A + \angle C = 180°, \angle B + \angle D = 180°$$

Here $\qquad 2x - 1 + 2y + 15 = 180°$
$$\Rightarrow 2x + 2y = 166$$
$$x + y = 83 \qquad \text{...(1)}$$

and $4x - 7 + y + 5 = 180°$
$$\Rightarrow 4x + y = 182 \qquad \text{...(2)}$$

Solving eqns (1) and (2), we get $x = 33$, $y = 50$
$$\angle A = 2x - 1 = 2 \times 33 - 1 = 65°$$
$$\angle B = y + 5 = 50 + 5 = 55°$$
$$\angle C = 2y + 15 = 2 \times 50 + 15 = 115°$$
$$\angle D = 4x - 7 = 4 \times 33 - 7 = 125°$$

13. **(B)**

Let x be the larger angle and y be smaller angle.

then $\quad x + y = 180° \qquad \text{...(1)}$

and $\quad x - y = 18°$

Solving eqns (1) and (2), we get
$$x = 99°, y = 81°$$

14. **(B)**

Let number of right answer be x and number of wrong answer be y.
$$3x - y = 40 \qquad \text{...(1)}$$
$$4x - 2y = 50 \Rightarrow 2x - y = 25 \qquad \text{...(2)}$$

Solving (1) and (2) $x = 15, y = 5$

No. of questions $= 15 + 5 = 20$

15. **(C)**

Let $₹x$ be the charge of full first class ticket and $₹y$ be reservation charge.
$$x + y = 216 \qquad \text{...(1)}$$
$$x + y + \frac{x}{2} + y = 327$$
$$\Rightarrow 3x + 4y = 654 \qquad \text{...(2)}$$

By solving eqns (1) and (2), we get

$x = 210, y = 6$

16. (A)

Let the number of rows be x and the number of students in each row be y.

Total number of students $= xy$

$$(x - 2)(y + 4) = xy$$
$$\Rightarrow \quad xy + 4x - 2y - 8 = xy$$
$$\Rightarrow \quad 4x - 2y = 8 \qquad \ldots(1)$$

and $(x + 4)(y - 4) = xy$

$$xy - 4x + 4y - 16 = xy$$
$$\Rightarrow \quad -4x + 4y = 16 \qquad \ldots(2)$$

From eqn. (1) and (2)

$$4x - 2y - 4x + 4y = 24$$
$$2y = 24 \Rightarrow y = 12$$

and $4x - 2 \times 12 = 8$

$$\Rightarrow \quad 4x = 8 + 24 = 32 \Rightarrow x = 8$$

Total no. of students $= 12 \times 8 = 96$.

17. (A)

Here $\sqrt{2}x - \sqrt{3}y = 0 \qquad \ldots(1)$

$\sqrt{5}\,x + \sqrt{2}\,y = 0 \qquad \ldots(2)$

then $2x - \sqrt{6}\,y = 0$; (1) $\times \sqrt{2}$

$\sqrt{15}\,x + \sqrt{6}\,y = 0$; (2) $\times \sqrt{3}$

Adding both equations $(2 + \sqrt{15})x = 0 \Rightarrow$ $x = 0$

Now $\sqrt{2} \times 0 - \sqrt{3}\,y = 0$

$\sqrt{3}\,y = 0 \Rightarrow y = 0$

Hence $x + y = 0 + 0 = 0$

18. (C)

Let the larger number be x and the smaller number be y.

Now according to question, $3x = 4y + 3$

$3x - 4y = 3 \qquad \ldots(1)$

and $7y = 5x + 1$

$5x - 7y = -1 \qquad \ldots(2)$

$21x - 28y = 21$

$20x - 28y = -4$

$$\underline{\quad - \qquad + \qquad + \qquad}$$
$$\underline{\qquad\qquad x = 25 \qquad\qquad}$$

and $3 \times 25 - 4y = 3$

$\Rightarrow 4y = 72 \Rightarrow y = 18$

$\therefore$ Smaller number $= 18$

19. (A)

Let one number be x

other number $= 8 - x$

$$\therefore \quad \frac{1}{x} + \frac{1}{8-x} = \frac{8}{15}$$
$$\Rightarrow \quad \frac{8 - x + x}{x(8 - x)} = \frac{8}{15}$$
$$\Rightarrow \quad \frac{8}{8x - x^2} = \frac{8}{15}$$
$$\Rightarrow \quad 8x - x^2 = 15$$
$$\Rightarrow \quad x^2 - 8x + 15 = 0$$
$$\Rightarrow \quad x^2 - 5x - 3x + 15 = 0$$
$$\Rightarrow \quad x(x - 5) - 3(x - 5) = 0$$
$$\Rightarrow \quad (x - 5)(x - 3) = 0$$
$$\Rightarrow \quad x = 5 \text{ or } x = 3$$

20. (A)

Let x litres of the 50% solution be mixed with y litres of 25% solution.

then $x + y = 10 \qquad \ldots(1)$

50% of x + 25% of y = 40% of 10

$$\Rightarrow \quad \frac{50x}{100} + \frac{25y}{100} = \frac{40 \times 10}{100}$$
$$\Rightarrow \quad 50x + 25y = 400$$
$$\Rightarrow \quad 2x + y = 16 \qquad \ldots(2)$$

From (1) and (2)

$$2x + 2y = 20$$
$$2x + y = 16$$
$$\underline{\qquad\qquad\qquad}$$
$$\underline{\qquad y = 4 \qquad}$$

$\therefore \qquad x = 10 - 4 = 6$

21. (A)

Let the fixed charges be ₹ x and other charges be ₹ y per km.

$x + 70y = 500 \qquad \ldots(1)$

and $x + 100y = 680 \qquad \ldots(2)$

Solving $30y = 180$

$\Rightarrow \qquad y = 6$

and $x + 70 \times 6 = 500 \Rightarrow x = 500 - 420$ $= 80$.

22. (A)

We have $\dfrac{1}{a}x + \dfrac{1}{b}y - (a+b) = 0$ ...(1)

$\dfrac{1}{a^2}x + \dfrac{1}{b^2}y - 2 = 0$ ...(2)

By cross multiplication

$$\dfrac{x}{\dfrac{a-b}{b^2}} = \dfrac{y}{\dfrac{a-b}{a^2}} = \dfrac{1}{\dfrac{a-b}{a^2b^2}}$$

$$x = \dfrac{a-b}{b^2} \times \dfrac{a^2b^2}{a-b} = a^2$$

and $y = \dfrac{a-b}{a^2} \times \dfrac{a^2b^2}{a-b} = b^2$

23. (B)

Let $\dfrac{1}{x} = u; \dfrac{1}{y} = v$

then $2u + 3v = 13$ ...(1)
and $5u - 4v = -2$ ...(2)

Solving $\dfrac{u}{-46} = \dfrac{v}{-69} = \dfrac{1}{-23}$

$\Rightarrow u = 2; v = 3$

$\therefore \dfrac{1}{x} = 2 \Rightarrow x = \dfrac{1}{2}; \dfrac{1}{y} = 3 \Rightarrow y = \dfrac{1}{3}$

24. (A)

$\dfrac{ax}{b} - \dfrac{by}{a} = a+b$ ...(1)

and $ax - by = 2ab$ ...(2)

Now $ax - \dfrac{b^2y}{a} = ab + b^2$

Solving $ax - by = 2ab$

$\Rightarrow y\left(b - \dfrac{b^2}{a}\right) = b^2 - ab$

$\Rightarrow y\left(\dfrac{ab - b^2}{a}\right) = b^2 - ab$

$\Rightarrow y = \dfrac{(b^2 - ab)a}{ab - b^2}$

$y = -a$

25. (B)

Given $\dfrac{x+y}{xy} = 2$

$\Rightarrow \dfrac{1}{y} + \dfrac{1}{x} = 2$ ...(1)

and $\dfrac{x-y}{xy} = 6 \Rightarrow \dfrac{1}{y} - \dfrac{1}{x} = 6$ ...(2)

Adding (1) and (2), we get

$\dfrac{1}{x} + \dfrac{1}{y} + \dfrac{1}{y} - \dfrac{1}{x} = 2 + 6$

$\Rightarrow \dfrac{2}{y} = 8 \Rightarrow y = \dfrac{2}{8} = \dfrac{1}{4}$

HOTS (ACHIEVERS SECTION)				
26. (C)	27. (B)	28. (C)	29. (C)	30. (B)

4. QUADRATIC EQUATIONS

Answer Key

1. (A)	2. (A)	3. (A)	4. (C)	5. (A)	6. (D)	7. (C)	8. (B)	9. (A)	10. (A)
11. (B)	12. (A)	13. (B)	14. (B)	15. (B)	16. (A)	17. (C)	18. (C)	19. (B)	20. (C)
21. (A)	22. (C)	23. (D)	24. (B)	25. (C)					

1. **(A)**

In order to find the values for y, we must set the equation equal to 0.

$2y^2 - 5y + 2 - 5 = 0$

$2y^2 - 5y - 3 = 0$

$(2y + 1)(y - 3) = 0$

$2y + 1 = 0 \qquad\qquad y - 3 = 0$

$2y = -1 \qquad\qquad\quad y = 3$

$y = -\dfrac{1}{2}; \; y = 3$

2. **(A)**

As I take a look at the answer choices, I know that I can eliminate letter C because that parabola opens down, and it must open up since the lead coefficient is positive.

If I factor this equation, I can find the x-intercepts to see which graph matches.

$0 = x^2 + 2x - 3$

$(x + 3)(x - 1) = 0$

$x + 3 = 0 \qquad\qquad x - 1 = 0$

Set the factors equal to 0

$x + 3 - 3 = 0 - 3 \qquad x - 1 + 1 = 0 + 1$

$x = -3 \qquad\qquad\qquad x = 1$

These are the x-intercepts.

Letter A and D both have x-intercepts of -3 and 1, so now it depends on the correct vertex. They both have an x-coordinate of -1, but different y-coordinates. Let's substitute -1 for x and see what we get for y.

$y = x^2 + 2x - 3$

$y = (-1)^2 + 2(-1) - 3$

$y = -4$

This means the vertex is $(-1, -4)$ and the graph of letter A is correct.

4. **(C)**

Discriminate $= b^2 - 4ac$ where: $a = 3$ $b = -5$ $c = 20$

$D = (-5)^2 - 4(3)(20) = -215$

Since the discriminate is negative, there are no real solutions.

5. **(A)**

In order to find the maximum height of the ball, I would need to find the y-coordinate of the vertex. Vertex formula: $x = -\dfrac{b}{2a}$ where: $a = -16$ $b = 36$ $c = 1.5$

$x = -\dfrac{36}{2(-16)}$

$x = 1.125$

Now substitute 1.125 for t into the equation and solve for h(t)

$h(t) = -16\,(1.125)^2 + 36\,(1.125) + 1.5$

$h(t) = 21.75$

10. **(A)**

The given equation is

$2x^2 + Px - 15 = 0$

$2(-5)^2 + P(-5) - 15 = 0$

$\Rightarrow \; 50 - 5P - 15 = 0$

$\Rightarrow \; -5P = -35$

$\Rightarrow \qquad P = 7$

$P(x^2 + x) + K = 0$

$\Rightarrow \; 7(x^2 + x) + K = 0 \Rightarrow 7x^2 + 7x + K = 0$

$\Rightarrow \; a = 7, b = 7, c = K$

$\therefore \;\; D = b^2 - 4ac = (7)^2 - 4(7)K = 49 - 28K$

The equation has equal roots

$D = 0 \Rightarrow 49 - 28K = 0 \Rightarrow K = \dfrac{49}{28} = \dfrac{7}{4}$

11. **(B)**

Given equation is

$3x^2 + 8x + 2 = 0$

and α, β are its roots then

$\alpha + \beta = \dfrac{-8}{3}, \; \alpha\beta = \dfrac{2}{3}$

$\therefore \;\; \alpha^2 + \beta^2 = (\alpha + \beta)^2 - 2\alpha\beta$

$= \left(\dfrac{-8}{3}\right)^2 - 2\left(\dfrac{2}{3}\right)$

$= \dfrac{64}{9} - \dfrac{4}{3} = \dfrac{64 - 12}{9}$

$= \dfrac{52}{9}$

12. (A)

The given equation is
$3x^2 + 11x + K = 0$

Let one root be α then other root is $\dfrac{1}{\alpha}$

$\therefore \quad a + \dfrac{1}{\alpha} = \dfrac{-11}{3}, \quad \alpha \cdot \dfrac{1}{\alpha} = \dfrac{K}{3}$

$\Rightarrow \quad 1 = \dfrac{K}{3} \Rightarrow K = 3$

13. (B)

Here $Kx^2 + 2x + 3K = 0$
then given Sum of roots = Product of roots

$\dfrac{-2}{K} = \dfrac{3K}{K} \Rightarrow \dfrac{-2}{K} = 3 \Rightarrow K = \dfrac{-2}{3}$

14. (B)

We have $3x^2 + 8x + 2 = 0$

and $\qquad \alpha + \beta = \dfrac{-8}{3}, \alpha\beta = \dfrac{2}{3}$

Now $\dfrac{1}{\alpha} + \dfrac{1}{\beta} = \dfrac{\beta + \alpha}{\alpha\beta} = \dfrac{\dfrac{-8}{3}}{\dfrac{2}{3}} = \dfrac{-8}{2} = -4$

15. (B)

The required equation is
$x^2 - $ (Sum of roots)$x + $ Product of roots $= 0$
$\Rightarrow \quad x^2 - [7 + (-3)]x + (7)(-3) = 0$
$\Rightarrow \quad x^2 - 4x - 21 = 0$

16. (A)

The equation $mx^2 + nx + p = 0$ has equal roots
then $\qquad n^2 - 4mp = 0 \Rightarrow 4mp = n^2$

$\Rightarrow p = \dfrac{n^2}{4m}$

17. (C)

Here $x^2 + px + 12 = 0$ has one root $a = 4$
$\therefore \quad 4^2 + p4 + 12 = 0$
$\Rightarrow p = -7$
Now the equation $x^2 - 7x + q = 0$ has equal roots

$(-7)^2 - 4\,(1)\,(q) = 0$ then
$\Rightarrow \quad 4q = 49 \Rightarrow q = \dfrac{49}{4}$

18. (C)

Here $x^2 - px + q = 0$
then $\quad \alpha + \beta = p, \ \alpha\beta = q$

$\left(-\dfrac{1}{\alpha}\right) + \left(-\dfrac{1}{\beta}\right) = \dfrac{-\alpha - \beta}{\alpha\beta} = \dfrac{-(\alpha + \beta)}{\alpha\beta} = \dfrac{-p}{q}$

$\therefore \quad \left(-\dfrac{1}{\alpha}\right)\left(-\dfrac{1}{\beta}\right) = \dfrac{1}{\alpha\beta} = \dfrac{1}{q}$

$\therefore \quad$ Required equation is $x^2 + \left(\dfrac{p}{q}\right)x + \dfrac{1}{q} = 0$

19. (B)

The given equation is
$x^2 - p(x + 1) - c = 0$
$\Rightarrow \quad x^2 - px + (-c - p) = 0$
$\therefore \quad \alpha + \beta = p$

and $\qquad \alpha\beta = \dfrac{-(c + p)}{1} = -(c + p)$

Now $\quad (\alpha + 1)(\beta + 1) = \alpha\beta + \alpha + \beta + 1$
$= -c - p + p + 1 = 1 - c$

20. (C)

Here $ax^2 + bx + c = 0$

then $\quad \alpha + \beta = \dfrac{-b}{a}, \ \alpha\beta = \dfrac{c}{a}$

Now $\quad (a\alpha + b)^{-2} + (ab + b)^{-2} = 1$

$\Rightarrow \dfrac{1}{(a\alpha + b)^2} + \dfrac{1}{(a\beta + b)^2} = 1$

$\Rightarrow \dfrac{(a\beta + b)^2 + (a\alpha + b)^2}{(a\alpha + b)^2(a\beta + b)^2} = 1$

$\Rightarrow \dfrac{a^2\beta^2 + b^2 + 2ab\beta + a^2\alpha^2 + b^2 + 2ab\alpha}{[(a\alpha + b)(a\beta + b)]^2}$

$\Rightarrow \dfrac{a^2(\alpha^2 + \beta^2) + 2b^2 + 2ab(\alpha + \beta)}{[a^2\alpha\beta + ab\alpha + ab\beta + b^2]^2} = 1$

$\Rightarrow \dfrac{a^2[(\alpha + \beta)^2 - 2\alpha\beta] + 2b^2 + 2ab(\alpha + \beta)}{[a^2\alpha\beta + ab(\alpha + \beta) + b^2]^2} = 1$

$$\Rightarrow \quad \frac{a^2\left[\left(\dfrac{-b}{a}\right)^2 - \dfrac{2c}{a}\right] + 2b^2 + 2ab \times \dfrac{-b}{a}}{\left[a^2 \times \dfrac{c}{a} + ab \times \dfrac{-b}{a} + b^2\right]^2} = 1$$

$$\Rightarrow \quad \frac{a^2\left[\dfrac{b^2 - 2ac}{a^2}\right] + 2b^2 - 2b^2}{\left[ac - b^2 + b^2\right]^2} = 1$$

$$\Rightarrow \quad \frac{b^2 - 2ac}{(ac)^2} = 1$$

$$\Rightarrow \quad b^2 - 2ac = a^2c^2$$
$$\Rightarrow \quad b^2 = a^2c^2 + 2ac$$
$$\Rightarrow \quad b = \pm\sqrt{a^2c^2 + 2ac}$$

21. (A)

We have $x^2 - px + q = 0$

Now $\alpha + \beta = p$, $\alpha\beta = q$

$\therefore \quad \alpha - \beta = 1$

$\quad 2\alpha = p + 1$

$\quad \alpha = \dfrac{p+1}{2}$

Now $\beta = p - \alpha = p - \dfrac{p+1}{2} = \dfrac{2p - p - 1}{2}$

$\qquad = \dfrac{p-1}{2}$

and $\qquad \alpha\beta = q$

$$\left(\frac{p+1}{2}\right)\left(\frac{p-1}{2}\right) = q$$

$$p^2 - 1 = 4q \Rightarrow p^2 - 4q = 1$$

22. (C)

The given equation is

$ax^2 + bx + c = 0$

$\alpha + \beta = -\dfrac{b}{a}$, $\alpha\beta = \dfrac{c}{a}$

$$\frac{1}{a\alpha + b} + \frac{1}{a\beta + b}$$

$$= \frac{a\beta + b + a\alpha + b}{(a\alpha + b)(a\beta + b)}$$

$$= \frac{a(\beta + \alpha) + 2b}{a^2\alpha\beta + ab\alpha + ab\beta + b^2}$$

$$= \frac{a \times \dfrac{-b}{a} + 2b}{a^2 \times \dfrac{c}{a} + ab \times \dfrac{-b}{a} + b^2} = \frac{-b + 2b}{ac - b^2 + b^2} = \frac{b}{ac}$$

23. (D)

Given a and b are roots of $x^2 + x + 1 = 0$

then $a + b = -1$ and $ab = 1$

$\therefore \quad a^2 + b^2 = (a + b)^2 - 2ab$

$\qquad\qquad = (-1)^2 - 2(1) = 1 - 2 = -1$

24. (B)

Let α be the non-zero common root.

then $\alpha^2 + 2\alpha + 3K = 0$

$2\alpha^2 + 3\alpha + 5K = 0$

$\therefore \quad K = \dfrac{-(\alpha^2 + 2\alpha)}{3}$

and $K = \dfrac{-(2\alpha^2 + 3\alpha)}{5}$

$$\Rightarrow \quad \frac{(\alpha^2 + 2\alpha)}{3} = \frac{(2\alpha^2 + 3\alpha)}{5}$$

$\Rightarrow \quad 5\alpha^2 + 10\alpha = 6\alpha^2 + 9\alpha$

$\Rightarrow \quad 6\alpha^2 + 9\alpha - 5\alpha^2 - 10\alpha = 0$

$\Rightarrow \quad \alpha^2 - \alpha = 0$

$\Rightarrow \quad \alpha(\alpha - 1) = 0 \Rightarrow \alpha = 0$ or $\alpha = 1$

when $\alpha = 1$ then $K = \dfrac{-(1^2 + 2 \times 1)}{3}$

$$= \frac{-(3)}{3} = -1$$

25. (C)

Given A and B are the roots of

$x^2 - 12x + 27 = 0$

$\Rightarrow \quad (x - 3)(x - 9) = 0$

$\therefore \quad$ A = 3, B = 9

Hence $A^3 + B^3 = 3^3 + 9^3 = 27 + 729 = 756$

HOTS (ACHIEVERS SECTION)

26. (B)	27. (B)	28. (C)	29. (C)	30. (B)

HINTS AND SOLUTIONS

Answer Key

1. (A)	2. (A)	3. (A)	4. (C)	5. (A)	6. (D)	7. (C)	8. (B)	9. (A)	10. (A)
11. (B)	12. (A)	13. (B)	14. (B)	15. (B)	16. (A)	17. (C)	18. (C)	19. (B)	20. (C)
21. (A)	22. (C)	23. (D)	24. (B)	25. (C)					

1. (A)

Let x be the first term and d be the common difference.

$$p^{th} \text{ term} = a \Rightarrow x + (p-1)d = a \qquad ...(1)$$
$$q^{th} \text{ term} = b \Rightarrow x + (q-1)d = b \qquad ...(2)$$
$$r^{th} \text{ term} = c \Rightarrow x + (r-1)d = c \qquad ...(3)$$

$$\therefore \quad a(q-r) + b(r-p) + c(p-q)$$
$$= x[q - r + r - p + p - q] + d[(p-1)(q-r)$$
$$+ (q-1)(r-p) + (r-1)(p-q)]$$
$$\Rightarrow a(q-r) + b(r-p) + c(p-q) = 0$$

2. (A)

Let the numbers be $a-d$, a, $a+d$.

$$a - d + a + a + d = 12 \Rightarrow 3a = 12 \Rightarrow a = 4$$
$$\text{and} \qquad (a-d)^3 + a^3 + (a+d)^3 = 288$$
$$a^3 - d^3 - 3ad(a-d) + a^3 + a^3 + d^3$$
$$+ 3ad(a+d) = 288$$
$$a^3 - d^3 - 3ad(a-d) + a^3 + a^3 + d^3$$
$$+ 3a^2d + 3ad^2 = 288$$
$$\Rightarrow 3a^3 + 6ad^2 = 288 \Rightarrow 3 \times 4^3 + 6 \times 4 \times d^2 = 288$$
$$\Rightarrow 24d^2 = 288 - 192$$
$$\Rightarrow d^2 = \frac{95}{24} = 4$$
$$\Rightarrow d = \pm 2$$

The numbers are, $4 - 2$, 4, $4 + 2 = 2, 4, 6$

3. (A)

Let a be the first term and d be the common difference.

$$a + 2d = 7$$
$$a + 6d = 3(a + 2d) + 2$$
$$a + 6d = 3a + 6d + 2$$
$$a - 3a = 2 \Rightarrow -2a = 2 \Rightarrow a = -1$$
$$\text{and } a + 2d = 7 \Rightarrow 2d - 7 - a = 7 - (-1) = 8$$
$$d = 4$$

$$\therefore \quad S_{20} = \frac{20}{2} [2 \times -1 + (20-1)4]$$
$$= 10 [-2 + 76] = 10 \times 74 = 740$$

4. (C)

Let a be the first term and d be the common difference.

$$S_m = \frac{m}{2} [2a + (m-1)d] = n$$
$$2am + m(m-1)d = 2n \qquad (1)$$
$$\text{and} \qquad S_n = \frac{n}{2} [2a + (n-1)d] = m$$
$$2an + n(n-1)d = 2m \qquad (2)$$

Subtracting (2) from eqn (1), we get
$$2a(m-n) + [(m^2 - n^2) - (m-n)]d = 2(n-m)$$
$$\Rightarrow (m-n)[2a + (m+n-1)d] = 2(n-m)$$
$$2a + (m+n-1)d = -2$$
$$S_{m+n} = \frac{m+n}{2} [2a + (m+n-1)d]$$
$$= \frac{m+n}{2} \times -2 = -(m+n)$$

5. (A)

$$a = 2, l = 50$$
$$\text{Now } S_n = \frac{n}{2}(a + l) \Rightarrow 442 = \frac{n}{2}(2 + 50)$$
$$\Rightarrow n = \frac{2 \times 442}{52} = 17$$
$$l = 2 + (17 - 1)d \Rightarrow \frac{50 - 2}{16} = d \Rightarrow d = 3$$

7. (C)

$$S_7 = 10, S_{14} = 10 + 17 = 27$$

8. (B)

Given $\dfrac{b+c-a}{a}, \dfrac{c+a-b}{b}, \dfrac{a+b-c}{c}$ are in arithmetic progression

$\Rightarrow \dfrac{b+c-a}{a}+2, \dfrac{c+a-b}{b}+2, \dfrac{a+b-c}{c}+$ 2 are in arithmetic progression

$\Rightarrow \dfrac{b+c+a}{a}, \dfrac{c+a+b}{b}, \dfrac{a+b+c}{c}$ are in arithmetic progression

$\Rightarrow \dfrac{b+c+a}{a(a+b+c)}, \dfrac{c+a+b}{b(a+b+c)}, \dfrac{a+b+c}{c(a+b+c)}$ are in arithmetic progression

$\Rightarrow \dfrac{1}{a}, \dfrac{1}{b}, \dfrac{1}{c}$, are in arithmetic progression

9. **(B)**

$t_n = 7 - 3n$

$t_1 = 7 - 3 \times 1 = 4 \Rightarrow a = 4$

$t_2 = 7 - 3 \times 2 = 1$

$d = 1 - 4 = -3$

$S_{25} = \dfrac{25}{2}\,[2 \times 4 + (25-1)\,(-3)]$

$\quad\quad = \dfrac{25}{2}\,[8 - 72] = -800$

10. **(B)**

Hint: The series is $105 + 112 + 119 \ldots + 994$

16. (b)

$a = 4, d = 7 - 4 = 3, t_n = 31$

$\therefore \quad t_n = a + (n-1)d$

$\Rightarrow 31 = 4 + (n-1)\,3 \Rightarrow n-1 = \dfrac{31-4}{3}$

$\Rightarrow n - 1 = 9 \Rightarrow n = 10$

12. **(C)**

Let a be the first term and d be common difference.

$\therefore \quad a + d = 8; a + 3d = 14$

$S_{30} = \dfrac{30}{2}\,[2 \times 5 + (30-1)3]$

$\quad\quad = 15\,[10 + 87] = 15 \times 97 = 1455$

13. **(C)**

Let a be the first term and d be the common difference

$t_m = \dfrac{1}{n}$

$\Rightarrow a + (m-1)d = \dfrac{1}{n}$ $\hspace{2cm}$ (1)

and $\quad t_n = \dfrac{1}{m}$

$\Rightarrow a + (n-1)d = \dfrac{1}{m}$ $\hspace{2cm}$ (2)

Subtracting eqn (2) from eqn (1)

$a + (m-1)d - a - (n-1)d = \dfrac{1}{n} - \dfrac{1}{m}$

$\Rightarrow d\,[m - 1 - n + 1] = \dfrac{m-n}{mn}$

$\Rightarrow d\,(m-n) = \dfrac{m-n}{mn} \Rightarrow d = \dfrac{1}{mn}$

and $\quad a = \dfrac{1}{mn}$

$\therefore \quad t_{mn} = \dfrac{1}{mn} + (mn - 1)\,\dfrac{1}{mn}$

$\quad\quad = \dfrac{1}{mn} + \dfrac{mn}{mn} - \dfrac{1}{mn} = 1$

15. **(B)**

Let a be the first term and d be the common difference

$\quad a + 7d = 31$

$\quad a + 14d = a + 10d + 16$

$\quad a + 14d - a - 10d = 16 \Rightarrow d = 4$

$\therefore \quad a = 31 - 7d = 31 - 28 = 3$

16. **(B)**

Here

$4k - 1 - (5k + 2) = (k + 2) - (4k - 1)$

$\Rightarrow \quad 4k - 1 - 5k - 2 = k + 2 - 4k + 1$

$\Rightarrow \quad\quad\quad -k - 3 = -3k + 3$

$\Rightarrow \quad\quad\quad\quad 2k = 6 \Rightarrow k = 3$

17. **(A)**

Let the numbers be $a - d, a, a + d$

Now $\quad a - d + a + a + d = 27 \Rightarrow a = 9$

and $\quad (a - d)\,a\,(a + d) = 405$

$\quad\quad a(a^2 - d^2) = 405$

$\quad\quad\quad 9(9^2 - d^2) = 405$

$\Rightarrow \qquad 81 - a^2 = 45$

$\Rightarrow \qquad d^2 = 36 \Rightarrow d = \pm 6$

The numbers are 3, 9, 15.

18. (C)

Let the numbers are $a - 3d$, $a - d$, $a + d$, $a + 3d$

$a - 3d + a - d + a + d + a + 3d = 50$

$\Rightarrow 4a = 50 \Rightarrow a = \dfrac{50}{4} = \dfrac{25}{2}$

$a + 3d = 4(a - 3d)$

$\Rightarrow a + 3d = 4a - 12d \Rightarrow 3a = 15d$

$\Rightarrow \qquad a = 5d$

$\Rightarrow \qquad \dfrac{25}{2} = 5d$

$\Rightarrow \qquad d = \dfrac{5}{2}$

$a - 3d = \dfrac{25}{2} - \dfrac{15}{2} = \dfrac{10}{2} = 5$

19. (A)

3, 7, 11, 15.....

$a = 3,\ d = 4,\ S_n = 406$

$S_n = \dfrac{n}{2} [2a + (n - 1)d]$

$\Rightarrow 406 = \dfrac{n}{2} [2 \times 3 + (n - 1)\,4]$

$\Rightarrow n[6 + 4n - 4] = 812$

$\Rightarrow 4n^2 + 2n = 812$

$\Rightarrow 2n^2 + n = 406$

$\Rightarrow 2n^2 + 29n - 28n - 406 = 0$

$\Rightarrow n(2n + 29) - 14(2n + 29) = 0$

$\Rightarrow (n - 14)(2n + 29) = 0$

$n = 14,\ n = -\dfrac{29}{2}$ (Not possible)

20. (A)

$S_1 = \dfrac{n}{2} [2 \times 1 + (n - 1)\,1]$

$\quad = \dfrac{n}{2} [2 + n - 1]$

$S_1 = \dfrac{n}{2} (n + 1)$

$\qquad S_2 = \dfrac{n}{2} [2 \times 1 + (n - 1)2]$

$\quad = \dfrac{n}{2} [2 + 2n - 2] = n^2$

$S_3 = \dfrac{n}{2} [2 \times 1 + (n - 1)\,3]$

$\quad = \dfrac{n}{2} [2 + 3n - 3] = \dfrac{n}{2} [3n - 1]$

Now $S_1 + S_3 = \dfrac{n}{2} [n + 1 + 3n - 1]$

$\quad = \dfrac{n}{2} \times 4n = 2n^2 = 2S_2$

21. (A)

Let a be the first term and d be the common difference

$a + 2d = 17$

$a + 6d = 27$

Solving these eqns we get $a = 12$

22. (C)

$t_k = 5k + 1$

$t_1 = 5 \times 1 + 1 = 6$

$t_n = 5n + 1$

$\therefore\ S_n = \dfrac{n}{2} [a + l] = \dfrac{n}{2} [6 + 5_n + 1]$

$\quad = \dfrac{n}{2} [5n + 7]$

23. (D)

$S_n = nP + \dfrac{1}{2} n(n - 1)Q$

$S_1 = P + \dfrac{1}{2} \times 1(1 - 1)Q = P$

$S_2 = 2p + \dfrac{1}{2} \times 2(2 - 0)Q = 2P + Q$

$S_2 - S_1 = 2P + Q - P = P + Q$

$P, P + Q \ ....$

Common difference $= Q$

24. (A)

$S_1 = \dfrac{n}{2} [2 \times 1 + (n - 1)1]$

$S_1 = \dfrac{n}{2} [2 + n - 1] = \dfrac{n}{2} (n + 1)$

$$S_2 = \frac{n}{2}\,[2 \times 2 + (n-1)\,3]$$

$$= \frac{n}{2}\,[4 + 3n - 3] = \frac{n}{2}\,[3n + 1]$$

$$S_m = \frac{n}{2}\,[2m + (n-1)(2m-1)]$$

$$= \frac{n}{2}\,[2m + 2mn - n - 2m + 1]$$

$$= \frac{n}{2}\,[2mn - n + 1]$$

$$S_1 + S_2 + \ldots + S_m$$

$$a = S_1 = \frac{n}{2}\,(n+1)$$

$$d = S_2 - S_1 = \frac{n}{2}\,[3n + 1 - n - 1]$$

$$= \frac{n}{2}\,[2n] = n^2$$

$$S_1 + S_2 + \ldots + S_m = \frac{m}{2}\,[S_1 + S_m]$$

$$= \frac{m}{2} \times \frac{n}{2}\,[n + 1 + 2mn - n + 1]$$

$$= \frac{mn}{2 \times 2}\,[2mn + 2]$$

$$= \frac{mn}{2}\,(mn + 1)$$

<table>
<tr><td colspan="5" align="center">HOTS (ACHIEVERS SECTION)</td></tr>
<tr><td>26. (C)</td><td>27. (B)</td><td>28. (D)</td><td>29. (D)</td><td>30. (D)</td></tr>
</table>

6. TRIANGLES

Answer Key

1. (A)	2. (B)	3. (A)	4. (B)	5. (B)	6. (B)	7. (A)	8. (A)	9. (C)	10 (A)
11. (B)	12. (C)	13. (B)	14. (B)	15. (B)	16. (A)	17. (A)	18. (A)	19. (C)	20. (C)
21. (B)	22. (A)	23. (A)	24. (B)	25. (A)					

1. (A)

In $\triangle PQR$ and $\triangle PST$

$\angle PST = \angle PQR$ $\quad\left[\begin{array}{l}\because ST\,||\,QR \\ \therefore \angle PST,\text{ and }\angle PQR\text{ are} \\ \text{corresponding angles}\end{array}\right.$

$\angle PTS = \angle PRQ$

$\therefore \triangle PST \sim \triangle PQR$

$\Rightarrow$ According to Thales' theorem

$$\frac{PS}{PQ} = \frac{PT}{PR}$$

Subtracting unity from both sides, we have,

$$\frac{PS}{QS} = \frac{PT}{RT} \Rightarrow \frac{7x-4}{3x+4} = \frac{5x-2}{3x}$$

$\Rightarrow 21x^2 - 12x = 15x^2 - 6x + 20x - 8$

$\Rightarrow 6x^2 - 26x + 8 = 0$

$\Rightarrow 3x^2 - 13x + 4 = 0$

$\Rightarrow 3x^2 - 12x - x + 4 = 0$

$\Rightarrow 3x(x-4) - 1(x-4) = 0$

$\Rightarrow (x-4)(3x-1) = 0$

$\Rightarrow x = 4,\ \dfrac{1}{3}\ \{x \neq \dfrac{1}{3}\text{ because } PS < 0\}$

$\therefore x = 4$

2. (B)

In $\triangle ABD$ and $\triangle ACD$

$$\frac{AB}{AC} = \frac{BD}{CD}$$

By Angle Bisector Theorem

$\dfrac{AB}{AC} = \dfrac{BD}{CD}$, it is given,

and $\angle BAC = 180 - 70 - 50$

$\qquad = 180 - 120 = 60°$

so, $\angle BAD = \dfrac{1}{2} \angle BAC$

$\qquad = \dfrac{1}{2} \times 60° = 30°$

3. **(A)**

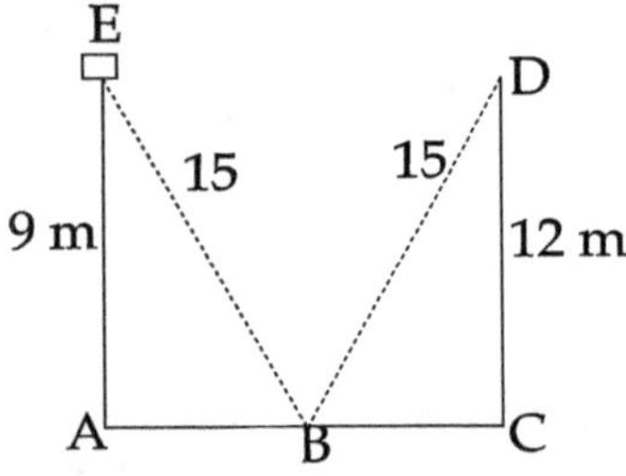

In $\triangle ABE$,

$\qquad AE^2 + AB^2 = BE^2$

$\Rightarrow 9^2 + AB^2 = 15^2$

$\Rightarrow AB^2 = 225 - 81$

$\qquad\quad = 144$

$\Rightarrow AB = 12$ m

Similarly,

In $\triangle BCD$

$\Rightarrow BC^2 = BD^2 - DC^2 = 15^2 - 12^2 = 9^2$

$BC = 9$m

$\therefore$ width of street = $(AB + BC) = 12 + 9 = 21$ m

4. **(B)**

$\because$ P and Q are mid-points of LM and LN respectively

$\therefore$ $PQ \parallel MN$ (according to midpoint theorem) and also,

$\dfrac{PQ}{MN} = \dfrac{LP}{LM} = \dfrac{LQ}{LN} = \dfrac{1}{2}$

$\therefore$ $\dfrac{\text{Area}(\triangle LPQ)}{\text{Area}(\triangle LMN)} = \dfrac{\frac{1}{2} \times PQ \times LG}{\frac{1}{2} \times MN \times LH}$

$= \left(\dfrac{1}{2}\right)^2 = \dfrac{1}{4}$, where G and H are feets of perpendicular dropped from L on PQ and MN respectively.

5. **(B)**

Ratio of areas = (ratio of altitudes)^2

$\qquad = \left(\dfrac{6}{9}\right)^2 = \dfrac{4}{9}$

6. **(B)**

$\angle CAB = \angle ACD$

$\qquad\qquad \{Alternate\ opposite\ interior\ angles\}$

$\angle BDC = \angle DBA$

$\therefore$ $\triangle AOB \sim \triangle COD$ (SS similarity)

$\therefore$ $\dfrac{\text{Area}(\triangle AOB)}{\text{Area}(\triangle COD)} = \left(\dfrac{AB}{CD}\right)^2 = \left(\dfrac{2CD}{CD}\right)^2$

$= 4:1$

7. **(A)**

$\angle CDO + \angle DCO = 115°$

$\Rightarrow \angle DCO = 115° - 70° = 45°$

$\angle OAB = 45°$ ($\because \triangle ODC \sim \triangle OBA$)

8. **(A)**

$CB = CD - BD = 11m - 6m = 5m$

$ED = AB = 12$ m

$\therefore AC = \sqrt{AB^2 + BC^2}$

$\qquad = \sqrt{12^2 + 5^2}$

$\qquad = \sqrt{169} = 13$ m

9. **(C)**

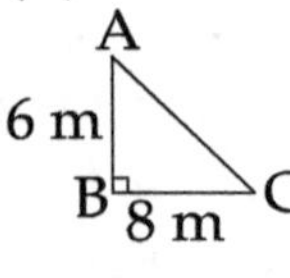

A is the point of cleavage *C* is the point where top of tree touches the ground

In $\triangle ABC$

$AB^2 + BC^2 = AC^2$ (Pythagoras' Theorem)

$6^2 + 8^2 = AC^2$

$\qquad\quad \Rightarrow AC = 10$ m

$\therefore$ Total (original) height = 10 m + 6 m

$= 16$ m

10. **(A)**

$\angle A = 180° - (\angle B + \angle C)$

$$= 180° - (55° + 35°) = 90°$$

∴ $\angle A$ is 90° or the triangle is right angled at A

∴ $AB^2 + AC^2 = BC^2$ (pythagoras' theorem)

11. (B)

Let the angles be $2x$ and $3x$ respectively

∴ $2x + 3x = 110°$

⇒ $5x = 110°$

⇒ $x = 22°$

∴ Angles are 44°, 66°, and 70°

12. (C)

In $\triangle ABC$

$\angle BAC = 180° - (100° + 40°) = 40°$

$\angle DAE = 180° - (50° + 40°) = 90°$ [linear pair]

13. (B)

Let the side of rhombus be x cm. Now, we know that the diagonals of rhombus bisect each other at right angles.

∴ By using Pythagoras' Theorem

$$x^2 = \left(\frac{16}{2}\right)^2 + \left(\frac{30}{2}\right)^2 = (8)^2 + (15)^2$$

$$= 64 + 225 = 289$$

⇒ $x = 17$ cm

∴ Perimeter $= 4 \times x = 4 \times 17 = 68$ cm

14. (B)

∵ Vertical angles of isosceles $\triangle$s are identical

∴ Other two equal angles of both the $\triangle$s will be identical.

∴ By using S-S-S similarity, we can say, that the two triangles are similar.

∴ Ratio of altitudes $= \sqrt{\text{Ratio of areas}}$

$$= \sqrt{\frac{225}{289}} = 15{:}17$$

15. (B)

∵ $BC \| DE$

∴ $\triangle ABC \sim \triangle ADE$

$$\begin{bmatrix} ∵ \angle B = \angle D & (corresponding) \\ \angle C = \angle E & angle \end{bmatrix}$$

∴ $$\frac{\text{Area of } \triangle ABC}{\text{Area of } \triangle ADE} = \left(\frac{BC}{DE}\right)^2$$

⇒ $$\left(\frac{25}{25+24}\right) = \left(\frac{BC}{14}\right)^2$$

[Ar $(\triangle ADE) = $ Ar$(\triangle ABC) + $ Ar$(\square BCED)$

⇒ $$\frac{BC}{14} = \frac{5}{7}$$

⇒ $BC = 10$ cm

16. (A)

$$\frac{\text{ar } (\triangle ABC)}{\text{ar } (\triangle PQR)} = \left(\frac{BC}{QR}\right)^2 = \left(\frac{9}{7}\right)^2$$

$$= \frac{81}{49}$$

17. (A)

In $\triangle ABC$

$AC^2 = AB^2 + BC^2$ (Pythagoras' theorem)

⇒ $AC = \sqrt{AB^2 + BC^2}$

$$= \sqrt{(10)^2 + (24)^2}$$

$$= \sqrt{676} = 26 \text{ m}$$

18. (A)

$\triangle ABC \cong \triangle APQ$

∴ $$\frac{BC}{PQ} = \frac{AC}{AQ} = \frac{BA}{AP}$$

⇒ $$\frac{8}{4} = \frac{AC}{AQ} = \frac{6.5}{3.25} \Rightarrow AC = \frac{6.5 \times 2.8}{3.25} = 5.6 cm$$

19. (C)

Both $\triangle$s are right angled, and also the elevation of coming sunlight will be same.

∴ All the angles of the $\triangle ABC$ and $\triangle PQR$ will be correspondingly identical.

∴ $\triangle ABC \sim \triangle PQR$

⇒ $$\frac{AB}{PQ} = \frac{BC}{QR}$$

$\Rightarrow \dfrac{12}{PQ} = \dfrac{8}{40}$

$\Rightarrow PQ = 12 \times 5 = 60\text{m}$

20. (C)

$\dfrac{AC}{BC} = \tan B$

$\Rightarrow \sqrt{3} = \tan B$

$\Rightarrow \angle B = 60°$

21. (B)

In $\triangle ABD$

$AB^2 = BD^2 + AD^2$

$\Rightarrow BD = \sqrt{AB^2 - AD^2}$

$\quad = \sqrt{13^2 - 5^2}$

$\quad = 12$ cm

$\because$ D bisects BC

$\therefore BC = 2 \times BD$

$\quad = 2 \times 12 = 24$ cm

22. (A)

$BD = \dfrac{BC}{2} = \dfrac{14}{2} = 7$ cm

[fig. is in the previous ques]

$\therefore AD^2 = AC^2 - AD^2$

$\quad = (25)^2 - (7)^2 = 576$

$\Rightarrow AD = 24$ cm

23. (A)

We know that if, $\triangle ABC \sim \triangle PQR$, then

$\Rightarrow \dfrac{AB}{PQ} = \dfrac{BC}{QR} = \dfrac{AC}{PR}$

or, Applying componendo and dividendo, it can be clearly seen that,

$\dfrac{\text{Perimeter}(\triangle ABC)}{\text{Perimeter}(\triangle PQR)} = \dfrac{AB}{PQ} = \dfrac{BC}{QR} = \dfrac{AC}{PR}$

$\Rightarrow \dfrac{25}{15} = \dfrac{9}{PQ}$

$\Rightarrow PQ = \dfrac{9}{25} \times 15 = 5.4$ cm

24. (B)

Ratio of perimeters = ratio of sides

$\qquad = \sqrt{\text{ratio of areas}}$

$\qquad = \sqrt{\dfrac{196}{169}}$

$\qquad = \dfrac{14}{13} = 14{:}13$

25. (A)

By angle bisector theorem,

$\dfrac{BD}{DC} = \dfrac{AB}{AC} \Rightarrow \dfrac{BD}{3} = \dfrac{5.6}{4}$

$\Rightarrow BD = \dfrac{3 \times 5.6}{4} = 4.2$

$BC = BD + DC = 4.2 + 3 = 7.2$ cm

HOTS (ACHIEVERS SECTION)				
26. (C)	27. (B)	28. (B)	29. (B)	30. (B)

7. CO-ORDINATE GEOMETRY

Answer Key

1. (A)	2. (A)	3. (B)	4. (D)	5. (A)	6. (A)	7. (A)	8. (B)	9. (D)	10. (B)
11. (B)	12. (B)	13. (B)	14. (B)	15. (A)	16. (B)	17. (A)	18. (C)	19. (A)	20. (B)
21. (B)	22. (A)	23. (B)	24. (A)	25. (C)					

1. **(A)**

A ————— P ————— B
(-2, 1)   (1, 2)   (7, 4)

Let the ratio be $k:1$.

$$1 = \frac{7k + 1(-2)}{k+1} \Rightarrow k+1 = 7k - 2$$

$$\Rightarrow 6k = 3$$

$$\Rightarrow k = \frac{3}{6} = \frac{1}{2}$$

2. **(A)**

Area of triangle

$$= \frac{1}{2}\Big[a(c+a-a-b) + b(a+b-b-c) \\ +c(b+c-c-a) \Big]$$

$$= \frac{1}{2}\big[a(c-b) + b(a-c) + c(b-a) \big]$$

$$= \frac{1}{2}\big[ac - ab + ab - bc + bc - ac \big]$$

$$= \frac{1}{2} \times 0 = 0$$

3. **(B)**

Area of triangle

$$= \frac{1}{2}\big[x_1(y_2 - y_3) + x_2(y_3 - y_1) + x_3(y_1 - y_2) \big]$$

$$= \frac{1}{2}\big[2(1-2) + (-2)(2+2) + 5(-2-1) \big]$$

$$= \frac{1}{2}\big[-2 - 8 - 15 \big] = \frac{25}{2} = 12.5 \text{ sq. units}$$

4. **(D)**

Let $P(x_1, y_1)$ and $Q(x_2, y_2)$ be the points

A   P   Q   B

$$x_2 = \frac{2(6) + 1(-3)}{2+1} = \frac{12-3}{3} = \frac{9}{3} = 3$$

$$y_2 = \frac{2(-7) + 1(5)}{2+1} = \frac{-14+5}{3} = \frac{-9}{3} = -3$$

or

$$x_1 = \frac{1(6) + 2(-3)}{1+2} = \frac{6-6}{3} = \frac{0}{3} = 0$$

$$y_1 = \frac{1(-7) + 2(5)}{1+2} = \frac{3}{3} = 1$$

$P(0, 1)$ and $Q(3, -3)$ are the required points

5. **(A)**

Let the other end be (x, y)

$$\frac{8+x}{2} = 4 \Rightarrow x = 8 - 8 = 0$$

$$\frac{10+y}{2} = 5 \Rightarrow y = 10 - 10 = 0$$

6. **(A)**

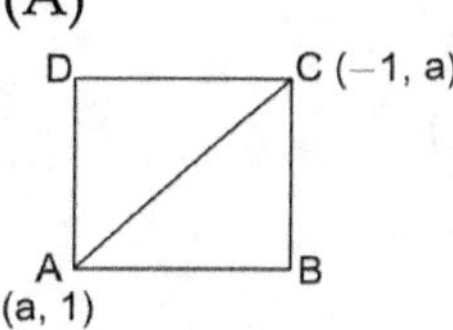

Let side of the square be x.

$$x^2 + x^2 = (-1 - a)^2 + (a - 1)^2$$
$$\Rightarrow 2x^2 = 1 + a^2 + 2a + a^2 + 1 - 2a$$
$$\Rightarrow x^2 = a^2 + 1$$
$$\Rightarrow 50 = a^2 + 1 \Rightarrow a^2 = 49$$
$$\Rightarrow a = \pm 7$$

7. **(A)**

Mid–point of $(4, 3)$ and $(-4, -3)$

$$= \left[\frac{4-4}{2}, \frac{3-3}{2} \right] = (0, 0)$$

$$0 = \frac{\frac{5}{\sqrt{2}} + x}{2} \Rightarrow x = \frac{-5}{\sqrt{2}}$$

$$0 = \frac{\frac{-5}{\sqrt{2}} + y}{2} \Rightarrow y = \frac{5}{\sqrt{2}}$$

8. **(B)**

$$\frac{2+1+x}{3} = 0 \Rightarrow x = -3$$

$$\frac{-4+3+y}{3} = 0 \Rightarrow y = 1$$

third vertex $= (-3, 1)$

HINTS AND SOLUTIONS

9. **(D)**

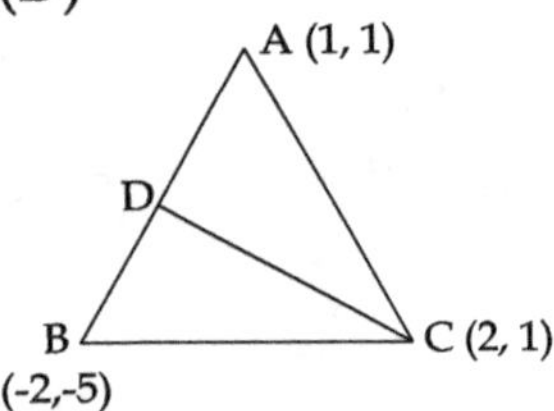

$$CD = \sqrt{\left(\frac{1}{2}-2\right)^2 + (-2-1)^2} \quad \left(-\frac{1}{2}, -2\right)$$

$$CD = \sqrt{\frac{25}{4}+9}$$

$$= \sqrt{\frac{25+36}{4}} = \frac{\sqrt{61}}{2}$$

10. **(B)**

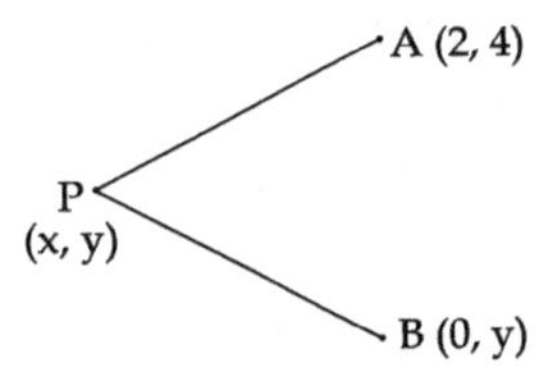

Let, the point be $P(x,y)$.
Given $AP = BP$
$$\Rightarrow AP^2 = BP^2$$
$$\Rightarrow (x-2)^2 + (y-4)^2 = (x-0)^2 + (y-y)^2$$
$$\Rightarrow x^2 + 4 - 4x + y^2 + 16 - 8y = x^2$$
$$\Rightarrow y^2 - 4x - 8y + 20 = 0$$

11. **(B)**

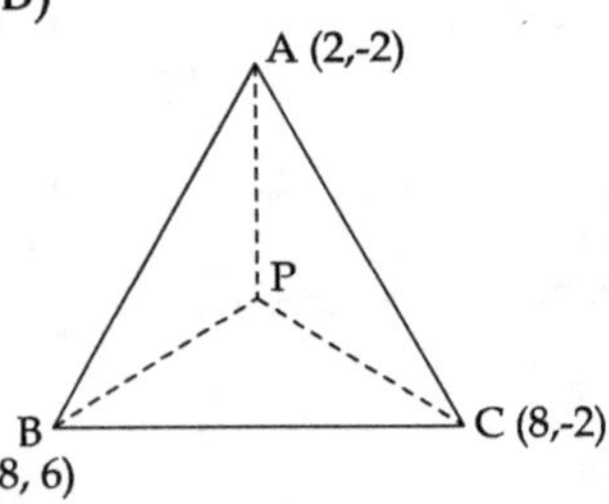

Let $P(x, y)$ be the circumcentre
$$PA = PB = PC$$
$$\Rightarrow PA^2 = PB^2$$
$$\Rightarrow (x-2)^2 + (y+2)^2 = (x-8)^2 + (y-6)^2$$
$$\Rightarrow x^2 + 4 - 4x + y^2 + 4 + 4y$$
$$= x^2 + 64 - 16x + y^2 + 36 - 12y$$

$$\Rightarrow -4x + 16x + 4y + 12y = 100 - 8$$
$$\Rightarrow 12x + 16y = 92 \Rightarrow 3x + 4y = 23 \quad ...(1)$$
and $PB^2 = PC^2$
$$\Rightarrow (x-8)^2 + (y-6)^2 = (x-8)^2 + (y+2)^2$$
$$\Rightarrow y^2 + 36 - 12y = y^2 + 4 + 4y$$
$$\Rightarrow 16y = 32 \Rightarrow y = 2$$
$$3x = 23 - 4 \Rightarrow 2 = 15 \Rightarrow x = 5$$
$$P(5, 2) \therefore PA = \sqrt{(5-2)^2 + (2+2)^2}$$
$$= \sqrt{9+16} = 5$$

12. **(B)**

$$\frac{x_1 + x_2}{2} = 3$$
$$\Rightarrow x_1 + x_2 = 6$$
$$y_1 + y_2 = 8$$
$$x_2 + x_3 = 2$$
$$y_2 + y_3 = 2$$
$$x_1 + x_3 = 4$$
$$y_1 + y_3 = -6$$

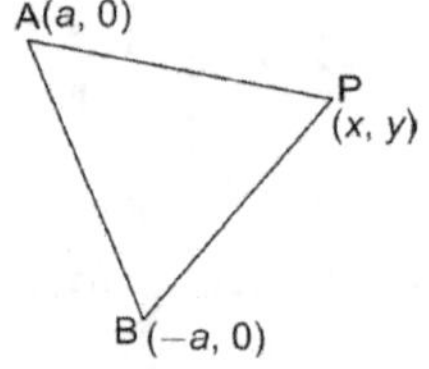

$$x_1 + x_2 + x_3 = \frac{12}{2} = 6$$
$$x_1 = 6 - 2 = 4; \ x_2 = 2, \ x_3 = 0$$
$$y_1 + y_2 + y_3 = 2$$
$$y_1 = 0; \ y_2 = 8; \ y_3 = -6$$
$$\text{Centroid} = \left[\frac{4+2+0}{3}, \frac{0+8-6}{3}\right]$$
$$= \left(2, \frac{2}{3}\right)$$

13. **(B)**

A(a, 0)

P (x, y)

B (−a, 0)

Here $(x-a)^2 + (y-0)^2 = 2c^2$
$$x^2 + a^2 - 2ax + y^2 = 2c^2$$
and $(x+a)^2 + (y-0)^2 = 2c^2$
$$\Rightarrow x^2 + a^2 + 2ax + y^2 + 2c^2$$
Now $x^2 + a^2 - 2ax + y^2 = x^2 + a^2 + 2ax + y^2$
$$\Rightarrow 4ax = 0 \Rightarrow x = 0 \text{ or } a = 0$$
$$(x-0)^2 + y^2 = 2c^2$$
$$\Rightarrow x^2 + y^2 = 2c^2$$

15. **(A)**

area of $\triangle ABC = 0$

$$\frac{1}{2}[a(b-1)+0(1-0)+1(0-b)] = 0$$

$$\Rightarrow ab - a - b = 0$$
$$\Rightarrow ab = a + b$$
$$\Rightarrow \frac{ab}{ab} = \frac{a}{ab} + \frac{b}{ab} \Rightarrow 1 = \frac{1}{b} + \frac{1}{a}$$

16. **(B)**

Distance of the point $(4, 7)$ from $(0, y)$
$= x$ co-ordinate $= 4$

17. **(A)**

Required Distance

$$= \sqrt{(\sin\theta - \cos\theta)^2 + (-\cos\theta - \sin\theta)^2}$$

$$= \sqrt{\begin{array}{c}\sin^2\theta + \cos^2\theta - 2\sin\theta\cos\theta + \cos^2\theta \\ + \sin^2\theta + 2\sin\theta\cos\theta\end{array}}$$

$$= \sqrt{2(\sin^2\theta + \cos^2\theta)} = \sqrt{2 \cdot (1)}$$

$$= \sqrt{2}$$

18. **(C)**

$(3 - 0)^2 + (0 - y)^2 = 5^2$

$9 + y^2 = 25 \Rightarrow y^2 = 16 \Rightarrow y = \pm 4$

y is positive, $\therefore y = 4$

19. **(A)**

$$\frac{a+b+c}{3} = 0 \Rightarrow a + b + c = 0$$

20. **(B)**

Area of triangle $= 10$

$$\Rightarrow \frac{1}{2}[a(6-1)+(-2)(1-2a)+3(2a-6)] = 10$$

$$\Rightarrow 6a - a - 2 + 4a + 6a - 18 = 20$$

$$\Rightarrow 15a = 20 + 20$$

$$\Rightarrow 15a = 40 \Rightarrow a = \frac{40}{15} = \frac{8}{3}$$

21. **(B)**

$$\frac{3x + 4 \times 2}{3 + 4} = -1$$

$$\Rightarrow 3x = -7 - 8 \Rightarrow 3x = -15$$
$$\Rightarrow x = -5$$

$$\frac{3y + 4 \times 5}{3 + 4} = 2 \Rightarrow 3y = 14 - 20$$

$$\Rightarrow 3y = -6 \Rightarrow y = -2$$

$$\therefore B = (-5, -2)$$

22. **(A)**

$\therefore$ Point is on y-axis

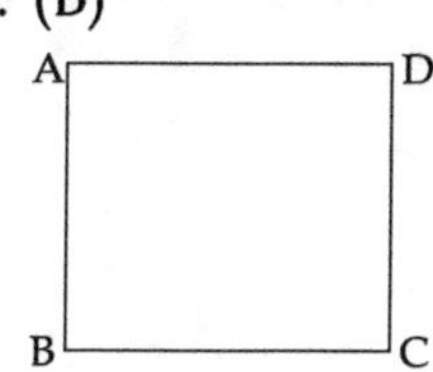

By section formula

$$0 = \frac{k(3) + 1(-4)}{k + 1}$$

$$\Rightarrow 3k - 4 = 0$$

$$\Rightarrow k = \frac{4}{3}$$

Ratio $= 4 : 3$

23. **(B)**

By distance formula, we get

$AB = BC = CD = DA$

and $AC = BD$

so, the given points are vertices of a square.

24. **(A)**

As point P is on x-axis, its co-ordinate $= (3, 0)$

25. **(C)**

$OP = 5$

$$\Rightarrow OP^2 = 25$$

$$\Rightarrow (x - 0)^2 + (4 - 0)^2 = 25$$

$$\Rightarrow x^2 + 16 = 25$$

$$\Rightarrow x^2 = 9 \Rightarrow x = \pm 3$$

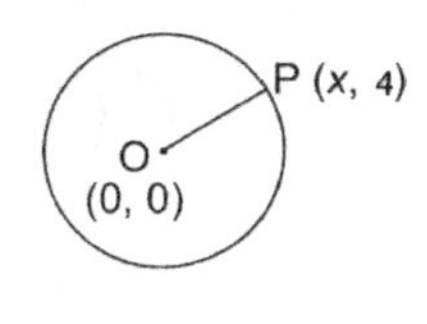

HOTS (ACHIEVERS SECTION)

26. (B)	27. (A)	28. (D)	29. (C)	30. (D)

HINTS AND SOLUTIONS

Answer Key

1. (A)	2. (B)	3. (A)	4. (D)	5. (D)	6. (D)	7. (D)	8. (C)	9. (A)	10 (D)
11. (B)	12. (A)	13. (A)	14. (D)	15. (D)	16. (B)	17. (B)	18. (A)	19. (B)	20. (A)
21. (B)	22. (C)	23. (C)	24. (B)	25. (D)					

1. **(A)**

Given A and B are complementary angles then

$$\angle A + \angle B = 90 \qquad \text{(i)}$$

and in $\triangle ABC \; \angle A + \angle B + \angle C = 180 \qquad \text{(ii)}$

From (i) and (ii) $\angle C = 90$

$\therefore \tan \angle C = \tan 90 = \infty$

2. **(B)**

Here $\sin \beta = \sqrt{1 - \cos^2 \beta} = \sqrt{1 - \left(\dfrac{4}{5}\right)^2}$

$$= \sqrt{1 - \frac{16}{25}} = \sqrt{\frac{9}{25}} = \frac{3}{5}$$

Now $\sin \alpha > \sin \beta \Rightarrow \alpha > \beta$

3. **(A)**

Given

$$\sin^2 20 + \sin^2 70 = \sin^2 20 + [\cos(90 - 70)]^2$$
$$= \sin^2 20 + \cos^2 20 = 1$$

4. **(D)**

Here $\sin \theta \cos(90 - \theta) + \cos \theta \cdot \sin (90 - \theta)$

$= \sin \theta \cdot \sin \theta + \cos \theta \cdot \cos \theta$

$= \sin^2 \theta + \cos^2 \theta = 1$

6. **(D)**

$$\frac{\sin^4 \theta - \cos^4 \theta}{\sin^2 \theta - \cos^2 \theta} = \frac{(\sin^2 \theta)^2 - (\cos^2 \theta)^2}{\sin^2 \theta - \cos^2 \theta}$$

$$= \frac{(\sin^2 \theta + \cos^2 \theta)(\sin^2 \theta - \cos^2 \theta)}{(\sin^2 \theta - \cos^2 \theta)}$$

$\sin^2 \theta + \cos^2 \theta = 1$

7. **(D)**

We have $(\sec \theta + \tan \theta)(1 - \sin \theta)$

$$= \left(\frac{1}{\cos \theta} + \frac{\sin \theta}{\cos \theta}\right)(1 - \sin \theta)$$

$$= \frac{(1 + \sin \theta)(1 - \sin \theta)}{\cos \theta} = \frac{1 - \sin^2 \theta}{\cos \theta} = \frac{\cos^2 \theta}{\cos \theta}$$

$= \cos \theta$

8. **(C)**

Given $a = \sec \theta - \tan \theta \qquad \text{(i)}$

and $b = \sec \theta + \tan \theta \qquad \text{(ii)}$

Multiplying (i) and (ii) we get

$\sec^2 \theta - \tan^2 \theta = a \times b$

$\Rightarrow 1 = ab$

$\Rightarrow a = \dfrac{1}{b}$

9. **(A)**

$\sec \alpha - \tan \alpha = m$ then

$\sec^4 \alpha - \tan^4 \alpha - 2\sec \alpha \tan \alpha$

$= (\sec^2 \alpha - \tan^2 \alpha)(\sec^2 \alpha + \tan^2 \alpha) - 2\sec \alpha \tan \alpha$

$= \sec^2 \alpha + \tan^2 \alpha - 2\sec \alpha \tan \alpha$

$= (\sec \alpha - \tan \alpha)^2 = m^2$

10. **(D)**

We have $\tan 15 \tan 20 \tan 70 \tan 75$

$= \tan 15 \tan 20 \tan (90 - 20) \tan (90 - 15)$

$= \tan 15 \tan 20 \times \cot 20 \cot 15$

$$= \tan 15 \times \frac{1}{\tan 15} \times \tan 20 \times \frac{1}{\tan 20} = 1$$

11. **(B)**

Given $\tan (A - 30) = 2 - \sqrt{3}$

$$\text{LHS} = \frac{\tan A - \tan 30}{1 + \tan A \cdot \tan 30}$$

$$\Rightarrow \frac{\tan A - \dfrac{1}{\sqrt{3}}}{1 + \tan A \cdot \dfrac{1}{\sqrt{3}}}$$

Now let $A = \dfrac{\pi}{4}$

then $\dfrac{\tan 45° - \dfrac{1}{\sqrt{3}}}{1 + \tan 45 \cdot \dfrac{1}{\sqrt{3}}}$

$\Rightarrow \dfrac{1 - \dfrac{1}{\sqrt{3}}}{1 + 1 \cdot \dfrac{1}{\sqrt{3}}} = \dfrac{\sqrt{3}-1}{\sqrt{3}+1}$

$= \dfrac{(\sqrt{3}-1)(\sqrt{3}-1)}{(\sqrt{3}+1)(\sqrt{3}-1)}$

$= \dfrac{(\sqrt{3}-1)^2}{3-1} = \dfrac{3+1-2\sqrt{3}}{2}$

$= \dfrac{4-2\sqrt{3}}{2} = 2 - \sqrt{3}$

Hence $A = \dfrac{\pi}{4}$

12. (A)

$\dfrac{\tan^3\theta - 1}{\tan\theta - 1} = \dfrac{(\tan\theta - 1)}{(\tan\theta - 1)}(\tan^2\theta + 1 + \tan\theta)$

$\qquad = \sec^2\theta + \tan\theta$

15. (D)

Given

$(\operatorname{cosec} A - \sin A)(\sec A - \cos A)$

$(\tan A + \cot A)$

$= \left(\dfrac{1}{\sin A} - \sin A\right)\left(\dfrac{1}{\cos A} - \cos A\right)$

$(\tan A + \cot A)$

$= \left(\dfrac{1-\sin^2 A}{\sin A}\right)\left(\dfrac{1-\cos^2 A}{\cos A}\right)(\tan A + \cot A)$

$= \left(\dfrac{\cos^2 A}{\sin A} \cdot \dfrac{\sin^2 A}{\cos A}\right)(\tan A + \cot A)$

$= (\cos A \sin A)\left(\dfrac{\sin A}{\cos A} + \dfrac{\cos A}{\sin A}\right)$

$= \cos A \sin A \dfrac{\left(\sin^2 A + \cos^2 A\right)}{\sin A \cos A}$

$= \sin^2 A + \cos^2 A = 1$

18. (A)

We have

$\dfrac{1}{1+\sin\theta} + \dfrac{1}{1-\sin\theta} = \dfrac{1-\sin\theta+1+\sin\theta}{(1-\sin^2\theta)}$

$\qquad\qquad = \dfrac{2}{\cos^2\theta} = 2\sec^2\theta$

20. (A)

Here

$\log \sin 0 + \log \sin 1 + \log \sin 2 + \ldots + \log \sin 90$

$= \log (\sin 0 \times \sin 1 \times \sin 2 \ldots \sin 90)$

$= \log (0) = 0$

21. (B)

$\sin^2 20 + \cos^2 160 - \tan^2 45$

$= \sin^2(180 - 160) + \cos^2 160 - \tan^2 45$

$= \sin^2 160 + \cos^2 160 - \tan^2 45$

$= 1 - 1 = 0$

22. (C)

We have $\dfrac{\sin\theta + \cos\theta}{\sin\theta - \cos\theta} + \dfrac{\sin\theta - \cos\theta}{\sin\theta + \cos\theta}$

$= \dfrac{\sin^2\theta + \cos^2\theta + 2\sin\theta\cos\theta + \sin^2\theta + \cos^2\theta - 2\sin\theta\cos\theta}{\sin^2\theta - \cos^2\theta}$

$= \dfrac{2}{\sin^2\theta + \sin^2\theta - 1} = \dfrac{2}{2\sin^2\theta - 1}$

$= \dfrac{2}{1 - \cos^2\theta - \cos^2\theta} = \dfrac{2}{1 - 2\cos^2\theta}$

$\therefore$ Both 1 and 2 are correct.

23. (C)

Length of the side (cm) of an equilateral triangle

$= 2 \times 8 \sin 60 = 2 \times 8 \times \dfrac{\sqrt{3}}{2} = 8\sqrt{3}$ cm.

24. (B)

We have $\dfrac{1+\sin\alpha}{1-\sin\alpha}=\dfrac{m^2}{n^2}$

$\Rightarrow \dfrac{1+\sin\alpha+1-\sin\alpha}{1+\sin\alpha-1+\sin\alpha}=\dfrac{m^2+n^2}{m^2-n^2}$

$\Rightarrow \dfrac{\cancel{2}}{\cancel{2}\sin\alpha}=\dfrac{m^2+n^2}{m^2-n^2}$

$\Rightarrow \sin\alpha=\dfrac{m^2-n^2}{m^2+n^2}$

25. (D)

Here $\sin\theta-\cos\theta=\dfrac{3}{5}$

Squaring both sides, we get

$\sin^2\theta+\cos^2\theta-2\sin\theta\cos\theta=\dfrac{9}{25}$

$\Rightarrow 1-2\sin\theta\cos\theta=\dfrac{9}{25}$

$\Rightarrow 2\sin\theta\cos\theta=1-\dfrac{9}{25}=\dfrac{16}{25}$

$\Rightarrow \sin\theta\cos\theta=\dfrac{8}{25}$

HOTS (ACHIEVERS SECTION)

26. (A)	27. (B)	28. (B)	29. (B)	30. (C)

9. CIRCLES

Answer Key

1. (A)	2. (A)	3. (A)	4. (A)	5. (A)	6. (B)	7. (A)	8. (B)	9. (A)	10 (A)
11. (B)	12. (B)	13. (A)	14. (A)	15. (B)	16. (A)	17. (A)	18. (A)	19. (C)	20. (A)
21. (C)	22. (B)	23. (A)	24. (C)	25. (B)	26. (A)	27. (B)	28. (D)	29. (A)	30. (B)

1. (A)

$\because\ EC=ED$

$\therefore\ \angle ECD=\angle EDC=62°$

$\therefore\ \angle DEC=180°-(2\times62°)=56°$

$\angle AEC=\angle DEB=\dfrac{180-56}{2}=62°$

$\therefore\ \angle AED=\angle CED+\angle AEC$

$=56°+62°=118°$

2. (A)

For any external point P,

$AP\times BP=PD\times PC$

$\Rightarrow (AB+BP)\times BP=12\times PC$

$\Rightarrow (8+10)\times10=12\times PC$

$\Rightarrow PC=\dfrac{180}{12}=15$ cm

3. (A)

$\because\ A, B, C$ and D are on the circumference of the circle.

$\therefore\ ABCD$ is a cyclic quadrilateral, i.e.,

$\angle A+\angle C=180°$

$\Rightarrow \angle A=180°-\angle C=180°-130°=50°$

$\therefore\ \angle DAB=50°$

4. (A)

In ΔOPT,

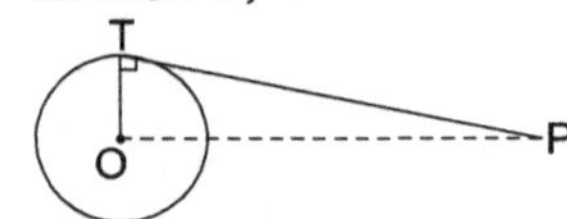

$OT^2+PT^2=OP^2$

$\Rightarrow PT=\sqrt{OP^2-OT^2}$

$=\sqrt{(17)^2-(8)^2}$

$=\sqrt{289-64}=\sqrt{225}=15$ cm.

5. (A)

Let r be the radius

$2\pi r=22$

$\Rightarrow r=\dfrac{22}{2\pi}=\dfrac{22\times7}{2\times22}=\dfrac{7}{2}$ cm

Area of quadrant $= \dfrac{1}{4} \times \pi r^2$

$$= \dfrac{1}{4} \times \dfrac{22}{7} \times \dfrac{7}{2} \times \dfrac{7}{2}$$

$$= \dfrac{77}{8} = 9.625 \text{ cm}^2$$

6. **(B)**

Diameter of the circumscribed circle

$$= \text{diagonal of the square}$$

$$= 10\sqrt{2} \text{ cm}$$

Radius $= \dfrac{10\sqrt{2}}{2} = 5\sqrt{2}$ cm

Area of circumscribed circle $= \pi r^2$

$$= \dfrac{22}{7} \times (5\sqrt{2})^2$$

$$= \dfrac{22}{7} \times 25 \times 2$$

$$= 157 \text{ cm}^2$$

7. **(A)**

Let the major arc be x cm.

Length of minor arc $= \dfrac{x}{5}$

Circumference $= x + \dfrac{x}{5} = \dfrac{6x}{5}$

$$\Rightarrow \quad \dfrac{6x}{5} = 2\pi r$$

$$\Rightarrow \quad \dfrac{6x}{5} = 2 \times \dfrac{22}{7} \times 10.5$$

$$\Rightarrow \quad x = 55 \text{ cm}$$

Required area $= \dfrac{1}{2} \times 55 \times 10.5$

$$= 288.75 \text{ cm}^2$$

8. **(B)**

Let r be the radius of the circle

$2\pi r - r = 37$

$$\Rightarrow \quad r\,(2\pi - 1) = 37$$

$$\Rightarrow \quad r\left(\dfrac{44}{7} - 1\right) = 37$$

$$\Rightarrow \quad r\left(\dfrac{37}{7}\right) = 37$$

$\Rightarrow \quad r = 7$ cm

Area $= \pi r^2 = \dfrac{22}{7} \times 7^2 = 22 \times 7 = 154 \text{ cm}^2$

9. **(A)**

Length of pendulum

= radius of the sector $= x$ cm.

Arc length = 8.8 cm

$$\Rightarrow \quad 2 \times \dfrac{22}{7} \times x \times \dfrac{30}{360} = 8.8$$

$$x = \dfrac{8.8 \times 360 \times 7}{2 \times 22 \times 30}$$

$$= \dfrac{88 \times 36 \times 7}{44 \times 30} = 16.8 \text{ cm}$$

11. **(B)**

Angle described by the minute hand in

35 minutes $= \dfrac{360}{60} \times 35 = 210^\circ$

$\theta = 210^\circ,\ r = 12$ cm

Area of the sector $= \dfrac{\pi r^2 \theta}{360}$

$$= \dfrac{22}{7} \times 12 \times 12 \times \dfrac{210}{360} = 264 \text{ cm}^2.$$

12. **(B)**

Radius of front of wheel = 40 cm

$$= \dfrac{40}{100} = \dfrac{2}{5} \text{ m.}$$

Circumference $= 2\pi \times \dfrac{2}{5} = \dfrac{4\pi}{5}$ m.

Distance moved by it in 800 revolutions

$$= \dfrac{4\pi}{5} \times 800 = 640 \text{ pm}$$

Circumference of real wheel $= 2\pi \times 1$
$= 2\pi$ m.

No. of revolutions $= \dfrac{640\pi}{2\pi} = 320$

13. **(A)**

$$BC = \sqrt{6^2 + 8^2} = \sqrt{36 + 64}$$

$$= \sqrt{100} = 10 \text{ cm}$$

(area $\triangle OAC$) + (area $\triangle OAB$) + (area $\triangle OBC$)

$$= \text{area } (\triangle ABC)$$

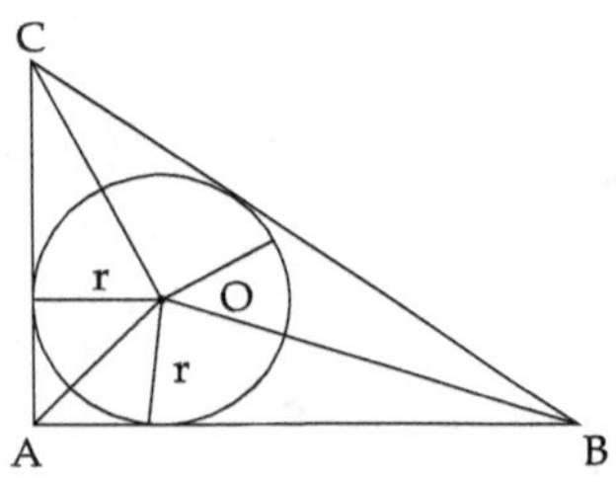

$$\Rightarrow \quad \frac{1}{2}\times 8\times r+\frac{1}{2}\times 6\times r+\frac{1}{2}\times 10\times r$$

$$=\frac{1}{2}\times 6\times 8$$

$$\Rightarrow \quad 8r+6r+10r=48$$
$$\Rightarrow \quad 24r=48 \Rightarrow r=2$$

14. **(A)**

Area of square = 484

Side of square = $\sqrt{484}$ = 22 cm

$\Rightarrow \quad 2\pi r = 22\times 4$

$\Rightarrow \quad r=\dfrac{22\times 4\times 7}{2\times 22}=14$ cm

Area of circle = πr^2

$$=\frac{22}{7}\times 14\times 14=44\times 14$$
$$=616 \text{ cm}^2$$

15. **(B)**

Area of the sector $OACBO$,

$$=\frac{\pi r^2\theta}{360}\text{cm}^2$$

$$=\frac{22}{7}\times\frac{14\times 14\times 90}{360}$$

$$=154 \text{ cm}^2.$$

Area of $\Delta OAB = \dfrac{1}{2}r^2\sin\theta$

$$=\frac{1}{2}\times 14\times 14\times\sin 90^\circ$$
$$=98 \text{ cm}^2$$

∴ Area of minor segment of circle
$$=154-98=56 \text{ cm}^2$$

16. **(A)**

Let R be the radius of outer circle and r be the radius of inner circle.

$2\pi R = 503$

$\Rightarrow \quad R=\dfrac{503\times 7}{2\times 22}=\dfrac{3521}{44}$

and $2\pi r = 437$

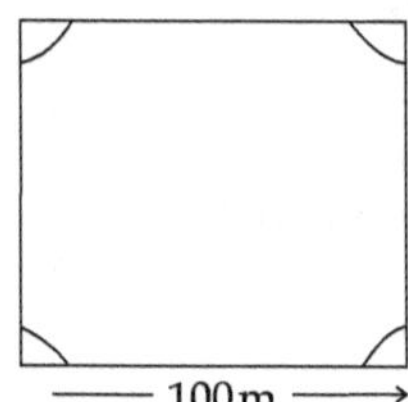

$\Rightarrow \quad r=\dfrac{437\times 7}{2\times 22}=\dfrac{3059}{44}$

Width of the track $= R-r=\dfrac{3521-3059}{44}$

$$=\frac{462}{44}=\frac{21}{2}\text{ cm}$$

Area of the track $= \pi(R^2-r^2)$
$$=\pi(R+r)(R-r)$$
$$=\frac{22}{7}\times\frac{6580}{44}\times\frac{21}{2}$$
$$=4935 \text{ m}^2$$

17. **(A)**

Area of the circular filed $=\dfrac{5775}{1.5}=3850 \text{ m}^2.$

$\pi r^2 = 3850$

$$r^2=\frac{3850\times 7}{22}=1225$$
$$r=35 \text{ m}$$

Circumference $= 2\pi r= 2\times\dfrac{22}{7}\times 35=220$ m

Cost of fencing $= 220\times 8.50 = ₹1870$

18. **(A)**

Let A be the area of each quadrant of the circle.

Radius of circle = 14 cm

$A=\dfrac{1}{4}\times\pi r^2=\dfrac{1}{4}\times\dfrac{22}{7}\times 14\times 14=154 \text{ m}^2.$

Area of 4 quadrants = 4 ×154 = 616 m²
Area of square park = (100)² = 10000 m²
Area of remaining part = 10000 − 616
$$=9384 \text{ m}^2$$

19. (C)

Area of the shaded region

= Area of square $ABCD$ – Area of two semicircles

$$= 14 \times 14 - 2\left(\frac{1}{2} \times \frac{22}{7} \times 7^2\right)$$

$$= 196 - 154 = 42 \text{ cm}^2$$

20. (A)

Area of the sector $= \frac{7}{20} \times \pi r^2$

$$\Rightarrow \frac{\pi r^2 \theta}{360} = \frac{7}{20} \times \pi r^2$$

$$\Rightarrow \theta = \frac{7 \times 360}{20} = 126°$$

21. (C)

$$2\pi r = 4 \times a$$

$$\pi r = 2a$$

$$r = \frac{2a}{\pi}$$

Area of circle $= \pi r^2$

$$= \pi \frac{4a^2}{\pi^2} = \frac{4a^2}{\pi}$$

Area of square $= a^2$

Ratio of their areas $= \dfrac{\dfrac{4a^2}{\pi}}{a^2}$

$$= \frac{4a^2}{\pi} \times \frac{1}{a^2} = \frac{4}{\pi} = \frac{4}{\frac{22}{7}}$$

$$= \frac{4 \times 7}{22} = \frac{14}{11} = 14 : 11$$

22. (B)

Let O be the centre of a circle of radius 5.2 cm. Let $OACBO$ be the sector with perimeter 16.4 cm.

$OA + OB + \text{arc } AB = 27.2$

$5.2 + 5.2 + \text{arc } AB = 16.4$

$\Rightarrow \text{arc } AB = 16.4 - 16.4 = 6 \text{ cm}$

Area of sector $OACBO$

$$= \frac{1}{2} \times \text{radius} \times \text{arc} = \frac{1}{2} \times 5.2 \times 6 = 15.6 \text{ cm}^2.$$

23. (A)

Speed $= 66 \text{ km/h} = 66 \times \dfrac{5}{18} \text{ m/s}$

$\therefore$ Distance moved in 10 min

$$= 66 \times \frac{5}{18} \times 60 \times 10 \text{ m}$$

In one complete revolution, distance moved

$$= \pi \times d$$

$$= \pi \left(\frac{80}{100}\right) \text{m}$$

Let it make h complete revolutions in 10 min.

$$\therefore \quad \pi \times \frac{80}{100} \times h = 66 \times \frac{5}{18} \times 60 \times 10$$

$$\Rightarrow h \times \frac{22}{7} \times \frac{80}{100} = 66 \times \frac{5}{18} \times 600$$

$$\Rightarrow h = \frac{5 \times 100 \times 7 \times 100}{80} = 4375$$

24. (C)

Distance moved by wheel

$$= 2 \times \pi \times r \times 5000 = 11000 \text{ m}$$

$$r = \frac{11 \times 7}{5 \times 2 \times 22} = \frac{7}{20} \text{ m}$$

$$= \frac{7}{20} \times 100 \text{ cm}$$

$$= 35 \text{ cm}$$

25. (B)

Let $PA = x$ cm

Then $OA = (9 - x)$ cm

$AP^2 = PR^2 - AR^2$

$AR^2 = 36 - x^2$

In $\triangle OAR$,

$OR^2 = AR^2 + OA^2$

$81 = 36 - x^2 + (9 - x)^2$

$81 = 36 - x^2 + 81 - 18x + x^2$

$18x = 36 \Rightarrow x = 2$ cm

$$AR = \sqrt{36-4} = \sqrt{32} = 4\sqrt{2}\,cm$$

$$\therefore QR = 8\sqrt{2}\,cm$$

area of PQR $= \dfrac{1}{2} \times 8\sqrt{2} \times 2$

$= 8\sqrt{2}\,cm^2$

26. (A)

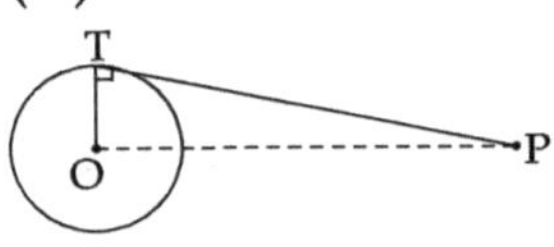

$$PT^2 + OT^2 = OP^2$$
$$\Rightarrow \quad PT^2 = (25)^2 - (7)^2$$
$$\Rightarrow \quad PT = \sqrt{576} = 24 \text{ cm.}$$

27. (B)

Area of bigger semi-circle

$= \dfrac{1}{2}(\pi r^2)$

$= \dfrac{1}{2} \times \dfrac{22}{7} \times 14 \times 14$

$= 22 \times 98 \text{ cm}^2 = 308 \text{ cm}^2$

Area of 2 small semicircles

$= 2 \times \left(\dfrac{1}{2} \pi \left(\dfrac{r}{2} \right)^2 \right)$

$= 2 \times \dfrac{1}{2} \times \dfrac{22}{7} \times \left(\dfrac{14}{2} \right)^2 = 154$

$\therefore$ Required area $= (308 + 154) \text{ cm}^2$

$= 462 \text{ cm}^2$

28. (D)

Distance moved by rope

$= (1.1) \times (60 + 28)$

$= 1.1 \times 88 = 96.8 \text{ cm}$

$\therefore$ No. of revolutions $= \dfrac{96.8 \times 100 \times 7}{22 \times 77} = 40$

29. (A)

$ABCD$ is a cyclic quadilateral

$(\angle B + \angle D = 180°)$

$\because \ AB \parallel CD$

$\angle A + \angle D = 180°$ (Alternate interior angles)

$\Rightarrow \angle D = 180° - 65° = 115°$

$\angle D + \angle B = 180° \Rightarrow x = 180° - 115° = 65°$

30. (B)

In $\triangle ABO$,

$\angle y + 25° + 100° = 180°$

$\Rightarrow \qquad\qquad y = 55°$

$\angle C + \angle A = 180°$ [$\because ABCD$ is cycle]

$\Rightarrow \qquad\qquad \angle C = 80°$

In $\triangle PBC$,

$\angle x + 55° + 80° = 180°$

$\Rightarrow \qquad\qquad \angle x = 45°$

HOTS (ACHIEVERS SECTION)

31. (B)	32. (A)	33. (C)	34. (A)	35. (A)

10. SURFACE AREA AND VOLUME

Answer Key

1. (A)	2. (B)	3. (B)	4. (C)	5. (C)	6. (A)	7. (B)	8. (B)	9. (A)	10. (A)
11. (B)	12. (B)	13. (B)	14. (B)	15. (A)	16. (C)	17. (A)	18. (A)	19. (D)	20. (A)
21. (A)	22. (A)	23. (D)	24. (A)	25. (B)					

1. (A)

Radius of cylinder = $\dfrac{12}{2}$ = 6 cm
height = 15 cm
Volume of cylinder = $\pi r^2 h$

$$= \dfrac{22}{7} \times 6^2 \times 15$$

$$= 540\pi \text{ cm}^3$$

Volume of 12 toys = 540 π cm³

Volume of 1 toy = $\dfrac{540\pi}{12}$ = 45 π cm³

Let the radius of the hemisphere be r cm.
Height of the cone = $3r$ cm
Volume of one toy = Volume of hemisphere
                    + volume of cone

$$= \dfrac{2}{3}\pi r^3 + \dfrac{1}{3}\pi r^2 \times 3r$$

$$= \dfrac{5}{3}\pi r^3$$

Now $\dfrac{5\pi r^3}{3} = 45\ \pi$

$\Rightarrow \qquad r^3 = \dfrac{45 \times 3}{5} = 27 = 3^3.$

$\Rightarrow \qquad r = 3$ cm

2. (B)

Let r be the radius of cylinder
Total surface area = $2\pi r\,(h + r)$

$\Rightarrow\ 2 \times \dfrac{22}{7} \times r(20 + r) = 2992$

$\Rightarrow\ 20r + r^2 = \dfrac{2992 \times 7}{2 \times 22} = 476$

$\Rightarrow\ r^2 + 20r - 476 = 0$

$\Rightarrow\ r^2 + 34r - 14r - 476 = 0$

$\Rightarrow\ r(r + 34) - 14(r + 34) = 0$

$\Rightarrow\ (r - 14)\,(r + 34) = 0$

$\Rightarrow\ r = 14;\ r = -34$ (Not possible)

diameter = 2 × 14 = 28 cm

3. (B)

Volume of the cube = 1728
$a^3 = 1728 \Rightarrow a = 12$ cm
Total surface area = $6a^2 = 6 \times (12)^2$

$= 6 \times 144 = 864$ cm²

4. (C)

Curved surface area of cylindrical pillar
= 264

$\Rightarrow\ 2\pi rh = 264 \Rightarrow h = \dfrac{264}{2\pi r} \qquad \text{...(1)}$

$\therefore\quad$ Volume = 924

$\pi r^2 h = 924 \Rightarrow h = \dfrac{924}{\pi r^2} \qquad \text{...(2)}$

From (1) and (2)

$$\dfrac{264}{2\pi r} = \dfrac{924}{\pi r^2}$$

$264r = 924 \times 2$

$h = \dfrac{924 \times 2}{2 \times 22 \times 7} = 6$ cm

5. (C)

Area of canvas = $2\pi rh + \pi rl$

$$= 2 \times \dfrac{22}{7} \times \dfrac{105}{2} \times 4 + \dfrac{22}{7} \times \dfrac{105}{2} \times 40$$

$$= 1320 + 6600 = 7920 \text{ m}^2$$

6. (A)

Radius of hemisphere = R

$\therefore\quad$ Volume of hemisphere = $\dfrac{2}{3}\pi R^3$

radius of spherical balls = $\dfrac{R}{4}$

Let the no. of spherical balls casted be x.

$\therefore\quad$ Volume of resulting spheres

$$= x\left[\dfrac{4}{3}\pi\left(\dfrac{R}{4}\right)^3\right]$$

Now,
Initial volume = Final volume,

$\therefore\quad \dfrac{2}{3}\pi R^3 = x \times \dfrac{4}{3} \times \pi \times \left(\dfrac{R}{4}\right)^3$

$\Rightarrow\ x = \dfrac{2}{4} \times 4 \times 4 \times 4$

$\Rightarrow\ x = 32$

7. (B)

Let the base areas and heights be A and h
respectively.

For cylinder, volume $= V_c = \pi r^2 h = Ah$

For cone, volume $= V_{co} = \dfrac{1}{3}\pi r^2 h = \dfrac{1}{3}Ah$

For hemisphere, volume $= V_h = \dfrac{2}{3}\pi r^3$

$$= \dfrac{2}{3}(\pi r^2)r$$

$$= \dfrac{2}{3}Ah \quad [\because h = r]$$

$\therefore$ Ratio of their volumes $= 1 : \dfrac{1}{3} : \dfrac{2}{3} = 3 : 1 : 2$

8. (B)

Let the number of cones made be n.

Volume of solid sphere = volume of resulting cones

$\Rightarrow \dfrac{4}{3}\pi(10.5)^3 = n \times \dfrac{1}{3} \times \pi \times (3.5)^2 \times 3$

$\Rightarrow n = \dfrac{4 \times (10.5)^2 \times 10.5}{(3.5)^2 \times 3}$

$= 12 \times 10.5 = 126$

9. (A)

Volume of given cylinder $= \pi r^2 h$

$$= \pi (12)^2 \times 16$$

Now,

$\dfrac{4}{3}\pi R^3 = \pi(12)^2 \times 16$

$\Rightarrow R^3 = \dfrac{12 \times 12 \times 16 \times 3}{4} \Rightarrow R = 12 \text{ cm}$

10. (A)

Let the thickness of the shell be t.

Inner radius $= r$, outer radius $= R$

$\therefore$ Volume of spherical shell

$$= \dfrac{4}{3}\pi(R^3 - r^3)$$

$$= \dfrac{4}{3} \times \pi \times (R^3 - 216)\,\text{cm}^3$$

$\therefore$ Weight of spherical shell

$$= \dfrac{4}{3} \times \pi \times (R^3 - 216) \times \dfrac{21}{1000}\,\text{kg}$$

$$= 11.176 \text{ kg}$$

$\Rightarrow R^3 = 343 \Rightarrow R = 7 \text{ cm}$

$\therefore$ Thickness $= t = (R - r) = (7 - 6) = 1 \text{ cm}$

11. (B)

Surface area of sphere $= 4\pi R^2$

If the radius of sphere is doubled, i.e., R becomes $2R$, then

New surface area $= 4\pi(2R)^2 = 16\pi R^2$

$$= 4\,(4\pi R^2)$$

$$= 4\,(\text{surface area})$$

$\therefore$ Surface area will become 4 times.

12. (B)

Ratio of volumes of spheres of radii r_1 and r_2 respectively

$$= \dfrac{\dfrac{4}{3}\pi r_1^3}{\dfrac{4}{3}\pi r_2^3} = \left(\dfrac{r_1}{r_2}\right)^3 .$$

Similarly,

Ratio of surface areas $= \dfrac{4\pi r_1^2}{4\pi r_2^2} = \left(\dfrac{r_1}{r_2}\right)^2$

According to condition

$\left(\dfrac{r_1}{r_2}\right)^3 = \dfrac{27}{8} \Rightarrow \dfrac{r_1}{r_2} = \dfrac{3}{2}$

$\therefore$ Ratio of surface areas $= \left(\dfrac{r_1}{r_2}\right)^2 = \left(\dfrac{3}{2}\right)^2$

$$= \dfrac{9}{4} = 9 : 4$$

13. (B)

Inner surface Area $= 4\pi r^2 = 324\,\pi \text{ cm}^2$

$\Rightarrow r^2 = \dfrac{324\pi}{4\pi}\,\text{cm}^2$

$\Rightarrow r = 9 \text{ cm}$

$\therefore$ Outer radius $= \sqrt{\dfrac{576\pi}{4\pi}}\,\text{cm}^2 = 12 \text{ cm}$

$\therefore$ Thickness of the shell $= (12 - 9) = 3 \text{ cm}$

14. (B)

Surface area of sphere $= 4\pi r^2 = 616$

$\Rightarrow r^2 = \dfrac{616}{4\pi} = \dfrac{616 \times 7}{22 \times 4} = 7 \times 7$

$\Rightarrow \quad r = 7$ cm

$\therefore \quad$ diameter $= 2r = 2 \times 7 = 14$ cm

15. (A)

Let the height of the required cone be h m

$\therefore \quad$ Required base area $= (16) \times 5$

$$= 80 \text{ cm}^2 = \pi r^2$$

Height $= h$ m

$$\text{volume} = \frac{1}{3}(\pi r^2)h$$

According to given condition

Total volume required $= 5 \times 100$ m³

$$= 500 \text{ m}^3$$

$$\Rightarrow \quad \frac{1}{3}(\pi r^2)h = 500 \text{ m}^3$$

$$\Rightarrow \quad h = \frac{500 \times 3}{16 \times 5} = 18.75 \text{ m}$$

16. (A)

Ratio of curved surface areas

$$= \frac{\pi r_1 l_1}{\pi r_2 l_2} = \frac{5}{4} \qquad \ldots\ldots(1)$$

$r_1 = r_2$

$\therefore \quad$ Ratio of slant heights

$$= \frac{l_1}{l_2} = \frac{5}{4} = 5:4 \text{ from (1)}$$

17. (A)

Ratio of volumes $= \dfrac{\pi r_1^2 h_1}{\pi r_2^2 h_2} = \left(\dfrac{r_1}{r_2}\right)^2 \dfrac{h_1}{h_2}$

$$= \left(\frac{2}{3}\right)^2 \times \frac{3}{2} = \frac{2}{3} = 2:3$$

18. (A)

We know that,

$$l = \sqrt{h^2 + r^2}$$

$$= \sqrt{(24)^2 + (7)^2}$$

$$= 25 \text{ cm}$$

Total surface area of cone

$$= \pi r (l + r)$$

$$= \frac{22}{7} \times 7 \times (25 + 7) \text{cm}^2$$

$$= 22 \times 32 \text{ cm}^2 = 704 \text{ cm}^2$$

19. (D)

Total surface area of cylinder

$$= 2\pi r (r + h)$$

$$= 2 \times \frac{22}{7} \times 14(14 + h)$$

$$= 88 (14 + h)$$

$$= 1760 \text{ cm}^2$$

$$\Rightarrow \quad h = \frac{1760}{88} - 14 = 6 \text{ cm}$$

$\therefore \quad$ Lateral Surface Area $= 2 \times \pi \times r \times h$

$$= 2 \times \frac{22}{7} \times 14 \times 6$$

$$= 528 \text{ cm}^2$$

20. (A)

Lateral surface area of canvas $= \pi r l$

Given, $\pi r^2 = 346.5$ m²

$$\Rightarrow \quad r^2 = \frac{346.5 \times 7}{22} \text{ m}^2 \Rightarrow r = 10.5 \text{ m}$$

$\therefore \quad l = \sqrt{h^2 + r^2}$

$$= \sqrt{(14)^2 + (10.5)^2} = 17.5 \text{ m}$$

$\therefore \quad$ Length of canvas needed

$$= \frac{\pi \times (10.5) \times (17.5)}{1.1}$$

$$= \frac{22 \times 10.5 \times 17.5}{7 \times 1.1}$$

$$= 30 \times 17.5 = 525 \text{ m}$$

21. (A)

Let the original radius be r and height be h.

Original volume $= V = \dfrac{1}{3}\pi r^2 h$

New radius $= 120\%$ of $r = \dfrac{120r}{100} = \dfrac{6r}{5}$

New height $= 120\%$ of $h = \dfrac{120h}{100} = \dfrac{6h}{5}$

New volume $= \dfrac{1}{3}\pi \left(\dfrac{6r}{5}\right)^2 \times \dfrac{6h}{5}$

$$= \frac{216}{125}\left(\frac{1}{3}\pi r^2 h\right) = \frac{216}{125}V$$

Increase in volume $= \dfrac{216V}{125} - V = \dfrac{91V}{125}$

$$\text{Increase \%} = \dfrac{91V}{125} \times \dfrac{1}{V} \times 100$$

$$= \dfrac{91V}{125} \times \dfrac{1}{V} \times 100$$

$$= \dfrac{91 \times 4}{5}$$

$$= 72.8\%$$

22. (A)

Given $\dfrac{2}{3}\pi r^3 = 19404$

where r is radius

$$\Rightarrow r^3 = \dfrac{19404 \times 3 \times 7}{2 \times 22} = (21)^3$$

$$\Rightarrow r = 21 \text{ cm}$$

Total surface area $= 3\pi r^2$

$$= 3 \times \dfrac{22}{7} \times 21 \times 21$$

$$= 4158 \text{ cm}^2$$

23. (D)

Let the radius of two spheres be R and r.

$$\therefore \dfrac{\dfrac{4}{3}\pi R^3}{\dfrac{4}{3}\pi r^3} = \dfrac{125}{216}$$

$$\Rightarrow \dfrac{R^3}{r^3} = \dfrac{5^3}{6^3} \Rightarrow \dfrac{R}{r} = \dfrac{5}{6}.$$

Ratio of their surface area $= \dfrac{4\pi R^2}{4\pi r^2} = \left(\dfrac{R}{r}\right)^2$

$$= \left(\dfrac{5}{6}\right)^2 = \dfrac{25}{36} = 25 : 36$$

24. (A)

Let the radii of two cylinders are $2r$, $3r$ and heights be $5h$ and $3h$.

Ratio of their volumes $= \dfrac{\pi (2r)^2 5h}{\pi (3r)^3 3h}$

$$= \dfrac{4 \times 5}{9 \times 3} = \dfrac{20}{27} = 20 : 27$$

25. (B)

Let l, b, h be the length, breadth and height

$$x = lb, \; y = bh, \; z = lh$$

$$\therefore \; lb \times bh \times hl = xyz$$

$$(lbh)^2 = xyz$$

$$lbh = \sqrt{xyz}$$

$$= \text{Volume of the cuboid}$$

HOTS (ACHIEVERS SECTION)

26. (B)	27. (C)	28. (B)	29. (D)	30. (A)

11. STATISTICS

Answer Key

1. (C)	2. (D)	3. (C)	4. (C)	5. (A)	6. (A)	7. (B)	8. (C)	9. (C)	10. (B)
11. (B)	12. (A)	13. (B)	14. (B)	15. (B)	16. (A)	17. (A)	18. (C)	19. (A)	20. (B)
21. (C)	22. (D)	23. (C)	24. (A)	25. (A)					

1. (C)

Given $\dfrac{6 + 7 + x + 8 + y + 14}{6} = 9$

$$\Rightarrow x + y + 35 = 54$$

$$\Rightarrow x + y = 19$$

2. (D)

Given

$$\dfrac{x + x + 3 + x + 6 + x + 9 + x + 12}{5} = 10$$

$$\Rightarrow 5x + 30 = 50$$

$\Rightarrow 5x = 20 \Rightarrow x = 4$

3. (C)

Here

Class	5-10	10-15	15-20	20-25	25-30	30-35	35-40	40-45
Frequency	5	6	15	10	5	4	2	2
c.f	5	11	26	36	41	45	47	49

$\therefore$ c.f. of $25 - 30 = 41$

4. (C)

The class having maximum frequency is called modal class i.e. 30–40.

5. (A)

The given data is ascending order is

8, 9, 11, 14, 15, 17, 18, 20, 22, 25

$n = 10$ (even)

$$\text{Median} = \frac{1}{2}\left[\frac{n}{2}th + \left(\frac{n}{2}+1\right)th\right]\text{ term}$$

$$= \frac{1}{2}\ [5^{th} + 6^{th}\text{ term}]$$

$$= \frac{1}{2}\ [15 + 17]$$

$$= \frac{1}{2}\times 32 = 16$$

6. (A)

$$\text{Mean} = \frac{\sum x_i f_i}{\sum f_i}$$

$$\Rightarrow 7.5 =$$
$$\frac{3\times 6 + 5\times 8 + 7\times 15 + 9P + 11\times 8 + 13\times 4}{6 + 8 + 15 + P + 8 + 4}$$

$$\Rightarrow 7.5 = \frac{18 + 40 + 105 + 88 + 52 + 9P}{41 + P}$$

$$\Rightarrow 307.5 + 7.5P = 303 + 9P$$

$$\Rightarrow 1.5P = 4.5 \Rightarrow P = \frac{4.5}{1.5} = 3$$

7. (B)

Class	0-10	10-30	30-60	60-80	80-90
f	5	15	30	8	2
cf	5	20	50	58	60

$N = 60$

$$\frac{N}{2} = 30$$

c.f just greater than 30 is 50

Median class is $30 - 60$

$$\text{Median} = 1 + \frac{\dfrac{N}{2} - F}{f}\times h$$

$$= 30 + \frac{30 - 20}{30}\times 30$$

$$= 30 + 10 = 40$$

8. (C)

The given data in ascending order is

41, 43, 57, 61, 71, 85, 92, 99, 127

$n = 9$ (odd)

$$\text{Median} = \left(\frac{9+1}{2}\right)^{th} = 5^{th}\text{ term} = 71$$

Required Difference $= 71 - 61 = 10$

9. (C)

The given data in ascending order is

5, 7, 9, 11, 13, 15, 17

$n = 7$ (odd)

$$\text{Lower quartile} = \frac{n}{4}th = \frac{7}{4}th = 2^{nd}\text{ term} = 7$$

$$\text{Upper quartile} = \frac{3n}{4}th = \frac{3\times 7}{4}th = \frac{21}{4}th$$

$$= 6^{th}\text{ term} = 15$$

$\therefore$ Sum $= 7 + 15 = 22$

10. (B)

The given data in ascending order is

0, 1, 1, 2, 2, 3, 3, 3, 4, 5

$n = 10$ (even)

$$\text{Lower quartile} = \frac{n}{4}th = \frac{10}{4}th = 2.5^{th}$$

$$= 3^{rd}\text{ term}$$

$$= 1$$

$$\text{Upper quartile } (Q_3) = \frac{3n}{4}th\text{ term}$$

$$= \frac{3 \times 10}{4} = 7.5^{\text{th}} \text{ term}$$

$= 8^{\text{th}}$ term

$= 3$

Interquartile range $= Q_3 - Q_1 = 3 - 1 = 2$

11. **(B)**

Here Mean $= \dfrac{\sum x_i f_i}{\sum f_i}$

$$= \frac{10 + 32 + 60 + 104 + 40 + 144 + 84 + 32}{5 + 8 + 10 + 13 + 4 + 12 + 6 + 2}$$

$$= \frac{506}{60} = 8.43$$

$N = 60$

$$\frac{N}{2} = \frac{60}{2} = 30 \text{ lies between } 24 - 36$$

Variate $= 8 \Rightarrow$ Median $= 8$

Required difference $= 8.43 - 8 = 0.43$

12. **(A)**

Given $\dfrac{1 + 2 + 3 + ... + n}{n} = 15$

$\Rightarrow \dfrac{\frac{n}{2}[1 + n]}{n} = 15$

$\Rightarrow \dfrac{1 + n}{2} = 15 \Rightarrow n = 30 - 1 = 29$

13. **(B)**

$\because$ Mode $= 3$ Median $- 2$ Mean

$\therefore 12 = 3$ Median $- 2 \times 24$

$\Rightarrow$ Median $= \dfrac{60}{3} = 20$

14. **(B)**

We have Mean $= \dfrac{\sum f_i x_i}{\sum f_i}$

$\Rightarrow 8.1 = \dfrac{132 + 5k}{20}$

$\Rightarrow 162 = 132 + 5k \Rightarrow 5k = 30$

$\Rightarrow \quad k = 6$

15. **(B)**

The given data in ascending order is

$25, 31, x - 3, 37, x + 4, 42, 43, 45, 46$

$n = 9$ (odd)

Median $= \dfrac{n + 1}{2} th$ term $= \dfrac{9 + 1}{2} th$ term

$= 5^{\text{th}}$ term

$\Rightarrow \quad x + 4 = 39$

$\Rightarrow \quad x = 35$

16. **(A)**

Values of x are 1, 2, 3, 4, 5, 6, 7

$n = 7$ (odd)

Median $= \dfrac{n + 1}{2} th$ term

$= \dfrac{7 + 1}{2} th = 4^{\text{th}}$ term $= 4$

17. **(A)**

First 5 natural numbers are 1, 2, 3, 4, 5

$n = 5$ (odd)

$\therefore$ Median $= \dfrac{n + 1}{2} th = \dfrac{5 + 1}{2} th = 3^{\text{rd}}$ term

$\Rightarrow$ Median $= 3$

1, 2, 3, 4, 5, 6

Median $= \dfrac{1}{2}(3 + 4) = \dfrac{7}{2} = 3.5$

Difference $= 3.5 - 3 = 0.5$

18. **(C)**

The variate having highest frequency is the mode.

19. **(A)**

Here Mean $= \dfrac{\begin{array}{l}0 + 2 + 2 + 3 + 3 + 3 + 4 + 5 \\ + 5 + 5 + 5 + 6 + 6 + 7 + 8 + 8\end{array}}{16}$

$= \dfrac{72}{16} = 4.5$

and $n = 16$ (even)

$\therefore$ Median $= \dfrac{1}{2}\left[\dfrac{16}{2}th + \left(\dfrac{16}{2} + 1\right)th\right]$

$= \dfrac{1}{2}[5 + 5] = \dfrac{10}{2} = 5$

also Mode $= 5$

20. (B)

The given data in ascending order is

1, 2, 3, 3, 3, 4, 5, 5, 6, 7

$\therefore$ Mean

$$= \frac{1+2+3+3+3+4+5+5+6+7}{10}$$

$$= \frac{39}{10} = 3.9$$

Mode = 3

Difference = 3.9 − 3 = 0.9

21. (C)

Class Interval	0-50	50-100	100-150	150-200	200-250	250-300
f	4	8	16	13	6	3
c.f	4	12	28	41	47	50
x	25	75	125	175	225	275

$$\therefore \text{Mean} = \frac{\sum x_i f_i}{\sum f_i} = \frac{7150}{50} = 143$$

22. (D)

Mean

$$= \frac{100+102+7f+80+72+60+77+72}{20+17+f+10+8+6+7+6}$$

$$\Rightarrow 7.5 = \frac{563+7f}{74+f}$$

$$\Rightarrow 555 + 7.5f = 563 + 7f$$

$$\Rightarrow 0.5\,f = 8$$

$$\Rightarrow f = \frac{8}{0.5} = \frac{8 \times 10}{5} = 16$$

23. (C)

$N = 8 + 10 + 11 + 16 + 20 + 25 + 15 + 9 + 6$

$= 120$

$$\therefore \frac{N}{2} = \frac{120}{2} = 60$$

60 lies in between 45 − 65

$\therefore$ Variate = 5

24. (A)

Class	0-10	10-20	20-30	30-40	40-50	50-60
f	5	8	20	15	7	5
c.f	5	13	33	48	55	60

$$N = 60; \quad \frac{N}{2} = \frac{60}{2} = 30$$

Median class = 20 − 30

$l = 20; \; F = 13; \; h = 10; \; f = 20$

$$\text{Median} = 20 + \frac{30-13}{20} \times 10$$

$$= 20 + \frac{17}{2} = 20 + 8.5 = 28.5$$

25. (A)

Class	3-6	6-9	9-12	12-15	15-18	18-21	21-24
f	2	5	10	23	21	12	3

Class 12 − 15 has maximum frequency.

12 − 15 is the modal class

$$\text{Mode} = l + \frac{f-f_1}{2f-f_1-f_2} \times h$$

$$= 12 + \frac{23-10}{2 \times 23 - 10 - 21} \times 3$$

$$= 12 + \frac{13}{46-31} \times 3$$

$$= 12 + \frac{13}{15} \times 3$$

$$= 12 + \frac{13}{5} = \frac{73}{5} = 14.6$$

HOTS (ACHIEVERS SECTION)

26. (B)	27. (B)	28. (D)	29. (D)	30. (B)

Answer Key

1. (A)	2. (B)	3. (C)	4. (A)	5. (B)	6. (B)	7. (A)	8. (A)	9. (A)	10. (A)
11. (B)	12. (A)	13. (C)	14. (B)	15. (A)	16. (A)	17. (A)	18. (B)	19. (A)	20. (C)
21. (C)	22. (A)	23. (A)	24. (A)	25. (A)					

1. (A)

1, 2, 3, ... 25

The numbers which are divisible by 4 are 4, 8, 12, 16, 20, 24

$$P \text{ (Number divisible by 4)} = \frac{6}{25}$$

P (Number not divisible by 4) $= 1 - \frac{6}{25} = \frac{19}{25}$

2. (B)

Total number of possible outcomes $= 36$

E = The sum of two numbers be 9 is as (3, 6), (6, 3), (4, 5), (5, 4)

$$P(E) = \frac{4}{36} = \frac{1}{9}$$

3. (C)

Total no. of tickets $= 20$

Let E = The ticket drawn has an even digit at 10's place

E = 180, 127, 122, 143, 222, 162, 182,

$$P(E) = \frac{7}{20}$$

4. (A)

Required probability $= 6000 \times 0.08 = 480$

5. (B)

Total no. of bulbs $= 24$

No. of defective bulbs $= 25\%$ of 24

$$= \frac{25}{100} \times 24 = 6$$

Now a bulb is drawn at random. It is found to be not defective and it is not put back. Now one bulb is drawn at random

from the rest. Hence the probability that this bulb is not defective $= \dfrac{17}{23}$

6. (B)

Total number of outcomes $= 350$

No. of score of 6 obtained $= 28$

No. of score under 6 obtained $= 350 - 28$

$$= 322$$

Probability of getting the score of under 6

$$= \frac{322}{350} = \frac{23}{25}$$

7. (A)

No. of possible outcomes $= 5 + 7 + 3 = 15$

Probability of black marble $= \dfrac{7}{15}$

Probability of white marble $= \dfrac{3}{15}$

Probability that the marble taken out will be black or white $= \dfrac{7}{15} + \dfrac{3}{15} = \dfrac{10}{15} = \dfrac{2}{3}$

8. (A)

Numbers are 1, 2, 3, ... 35

Total no. of possible outcomes $= 35$

E = The number is a multiple of 7

$\quad$ = 7, 14, 21, 28, 35

$$P(E) = \frac{5}{35} = \frac{1}{7}$$

P (Not a multiple of 7) $= 1 - \dfrac{1}{7} = \dfrac{6}{7}$

9. (A)

Total no. of balls $= 6 + 8 + 5 + 3 = 22$

Probability that ball drawn is not white

$$= \frac{6+5+3}{22} = \frac{14}{22} = \frac{7}{11}$$

10. (A)

Total no. of students $= 35 + 15 = 50$

Probability that selected student is a girl

$$= \frac{15}{50} = \frac{3}{10}$$

11. (B)

In a leap year, there are 366 days. There are 52 weeks and 2 days. There are 52 Sundays. There may be five possibilities of being not a Sunday, which are (Monday, Tuesday) (Tuesday, Wednesday), (Wednesday, Thursday), (Thursday, Friday), (Friday, Saturday).

Probability for 52 Sunday $= \dfrac{5}{7}$

12. (A)

Let no. of white balls $= x$

Total no. of balls $= 6 + 4 + x = 10 + x$

Probability of not drawing a white ball

$$= \frac{4+6}{10+x} = \frac{10}{10+x}$$

$$\frac{10}{10+x} = \frac{2}{3} \text{ (given)}$$

$$\Rightarrow 20 + 2x = 30$$

$$2x = 30 - 20 \Rightarrow 2x = 10$$

$$\Rightarrow x = 5$$

13. (C)

Let the no. of black balls $= x$

Total no. of balls $= x + 5$

Probability of drawing a black ball $= \dfrac{x}{5+x}$

Probability of drawing a red ball $= \dfrac{5}{5+x}$

According to question,

$$\frac{x}{5+x} = \frac{2 \times 5}{5+x} \Rightarrow x = 10$$

14. (B)

Remaining cards $= 52 - 4 = 48$

There are 3 kings

$$\therefore \ P \text{ (getting a king)} = \frac{3}{48} = \frac{1}{16}$$

15. (A)

Total no. of outcomes $= 52$

No. of ace cards $= 4$

No. of Non ace cards $= 52 - 4 = 48$

$$P \text{ (getting a non-ace card)} = \frac{48}{52} = \frac{12}{13}$$

16. (A)

Let there be b blue, g green and w white marbles.

$$b + g + w = 54$$

$$P \text{ (getting a blue marble)} = \frac{b}{54}$$

$$\Rightarrow \frac{1}{3} = \frac{b}{54} \Rightarrow b = 18$$

$$P \text{ (getting a green marble)}$$

$$= \frac{4}{9} \Rightarrow \frac{4}{9} = \frac{g}{54} \Rightarrow g = 24$$

No. of while marbles

$$= 54 - (18 + 24) = 54 - 42 = 12$$

17. (A)

Two numbers can be selected in 9 ways (1, 2), (1, 5), (1, 7) (2, 2) (2, 5), (2, 7), (3, 2) (3, 5), (3, 7)

Total no. of possible outcomes $= 9$

Favourable no. of outcomes $= 7$

$$P \text{ (getting a product less than 15)} = \frac{7}{9}$$

18. (B)

Total no. of possible outcomes

$$= 70 + 30 + 50$$

$$= 150$$

No. of ₹5 coin $= 50$

No. of coins of ₹1 & ₹2 coin $= 70 + 30 = 100$

$$P \text{ (will not be ₹5 coin)} = \frac{100}{150} = \frac{2}{3}$$

19. **(A)**

Total no. of possible outcomes = 7

$x^2 < 12$

P (getting that $x^2 < 12$) = $\dfrac{6}{7}$

20. **(C)**

Total no. of letters = 13

No. of vowel letters = 6

Required probability = $\dfrac{6}{13}$

21. **(C)**

Total no. of balls = $7 + 8 + 4 + 5 = 24$

The no. of balls which are not green

$= 7 + 4 + 5 = 16$

P (not getting a green ball) = $\dfrac{16}{24} = \dfrac{2}{3}$

22. **(A)**

Total no. of letters = 13

No. of consonant letters = 8

Required probability = $\dfrac{8}{13}$

23. **(A)**

Total no. of ways Pravin & Navin may have their birthday = 365×365

No. of ways in which they have the same birthday = 365

Required probability = $\dfrac{365}{365 \times 365} = \dfrac{1}{365}$

24. **(A)**

Total no. of tickets = 500

Total no. of prizes = 15

P (win a prize) = $\dfrac{15}{500} = \dfrac{3}{100} = 0.03$

25. **(A)**

Total no. of possible outcomes = 600

No. of defective shirts = 12

No. of non-defective shirts = $600 - 12 = 588$

Required probability = $\dfrac{588}{600} = \dfrac{49}{50} = 0.98$

HOTS (ACHIEVERS SECTION)

26. (A)	27. (C)	28. (C)	29. (A)	30. (C)

13. LOGICAL REASONING

Answer Key

1. (B)	2. (C)	3. (C)	4. (C)	5. (C)	6. (D)	7. (C)	8. (B)	9. (D)	10. (A)
11. (B)	12. (D)	13. (B)	14. (D)	15. (C)	16. (C)	17. (A)	18. (C)	19. (B)	20. (B)
21. (C)	22. (E)	23. (B)	24. (C)	25. (C)	26. (A)	27. (C)	28. (B)	29. (D)	30. (B)
31. (D)	32. (B)	33. (D)	34. (C)	35. (D)					

1. **(C)**

$2836 = 2 + 8 - 3 + 6 = 13$

$9423 = 9 + 4 - 2 + 3 = 14$

$7229 = 7 + 2 - 2 + 9 = 16$

2. **(B)**

$\left. \begin{array}{l} 211 \Rightarrow 2 + 1 + 1 = 4 \\ 333 \Rightarrow 3 + 3 + 3 = 9 \end{array} \right] + 5t$

Similarly

$\left. \begin{array}{l} 356 \Rightarrow 3 + 5 + 6 = 14 \\ 388 \Rightarrow 3 + 8 + 8 = 19 \end{array} \right] + 5$

3. **(A)**

TSR : FED :: WVU : MLK

4. **(B)**

Except whale, all are reptiles.

5. **(D)**

Except ornament, all are different kinds of ornaments.

6. **(A)**

All others are continents.

7. **(C)**

Here,

C	O	M	E
$-1\downarrow$	$-1\downarrow$	$-1\downarrow$	$-1\downarrow$
B	N	L	D

Then,

B	R	I	N	G
$\downarrow-1$	$\downarrow-1$	$\downarrow-1$	$\downarrow-1$	$\downarrow-1$
A	Q	H	M	F

$\Rightarrow$

8. **(A)**

By reversing the order

Here   SILVER $\rightarrow$ REVLIS

Similarly   BLACK $\rightarrow$ KCALB

9. **(D)**

Given,

R	O	P	E		A	P	P	L	E
$\downarrow$	$\downarrow$	$\downarrow$	$\downarrow$		$\downarrow$	$\downarrow$	$\downarrow$	$\downarrow$	$\downarrow$
3	4	5	6		1	5	5	2	6

then Direct substitution,

$5 \rightarrow P$ $4 \rightarrow O$ $6 \rightarrow E$ $1 \rightarrow A$ $3 \rightarrow R$

Hence, $54613 \rightarrow$ POEAR

10. **(B)**

7th day of a month is three days earlier than Friday that is Tuesday

14th day is Tuesday

19th day is Sunday.

11. **(A)**

Given P is 18th from the front. R is 25th

Number of persons between P and $R = 6$

R is exactly the middle of P and Q.

and. No. of persons between R and $Q = 6$

Hence $\xleftarrow{17} P \xleftarrow{6} R \xleftarrow{6} Q \xleftarrow{15}$

number of persons in the queue

$= 17 + 1 + 6 + 1 + 6 + 1 + 15 = 47$

12. **(C)**

On subtracting 3 from the middle digit the numbers become

559, 332, 524, 341, 412

Now reversing the positions of digits,

955, 233, 425, 143, 214

Arranging the above numbers in descending order, we get

955. 425, , 214, 143

Middle No.

Hence 3 is required number.

13. **(D)**

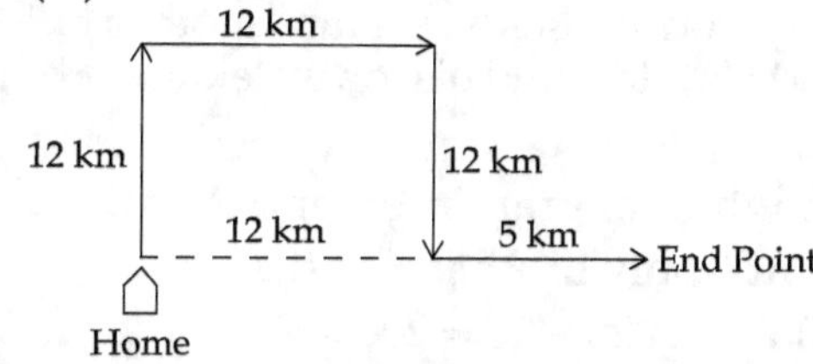

Distance $= 12 + 5 = 17$ km in East direction

14. **(C)**

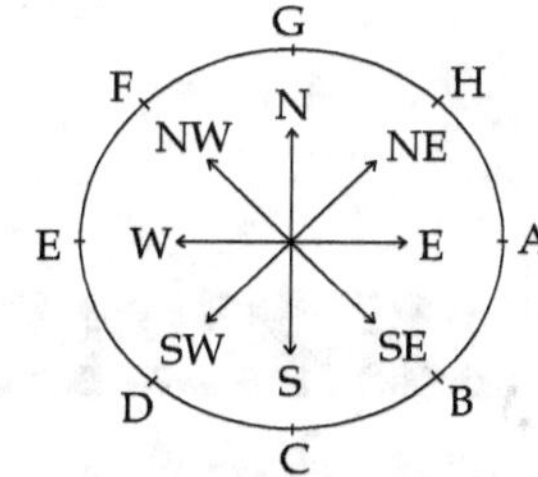

Position of D is South–West.

15. **(C)**

The movement of Dinesh is as given below

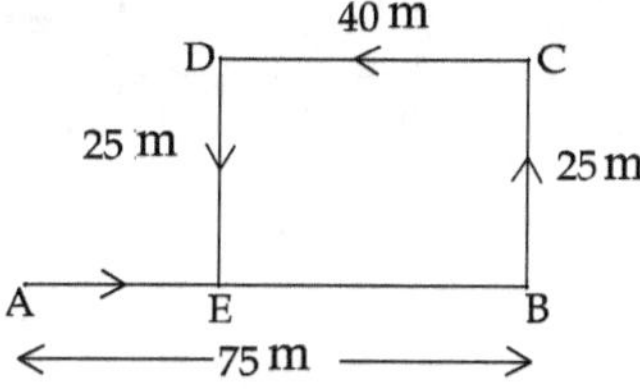

From above fig. $EB = DC = 40$m

Dinesh's distance from the starting point A

$= AE = AB - EB$

$= 75 - 40 = 35$ m

16. (A)
Because *E* is not present in the given word.

17. (D)
Because there is only one *E* in the given word.

18. (B)
Because *N* is not present in the given word.

19. (B)
Punam's mother Mamta is the youngest sister of Mishra and sister of Prabhat. Prabhat is Punam's uncle.

20. (D)
Only son of Rekha's grandmother means Rekha's father and his son is Rekha's brother.

21. (A)
Daughter of grandmother = Aunt.
Aunt's only brother = Father

22. (C) Given $20 - 10 = 200$
but $20 \times 10 = 200$; $-$ stands for $\times$.
Given $8 \div 4 = 12$ but $8 + 4 = 12$
$\therefore \div$ stands for $+$
Given $6 \times 2 = 4$ but $6 - 2 = 4$
$\therefore \times$ stands for $-$

Given expression
$= 100 - 10 \times 1000 \div 1000 + 100 \times 10$
$= 100 \times 10 - 1000 + 1000 \div 100 - 10$
$= 1000 - 1000 + 1000 \div 100 - 10$
$= 1000 - 1000 + 10 - 10$
$= 0 + 0 = 0$

23. (d) We have $(10\ C\ 4)\ A\ (4\ C\ 4)\ B\ 6$
$= (10 \times 4) + (4 \times 4) - 6 = 40 + 16 - 6 = 50$

24. (a) Using correct symbols, we have
$(3 \times 15 + 19) \div 8 - 6$
$= (45 + 19) \div 8 - 6$
$= 64 \div 8 - 6 = 8 - 6 = 2$

25. (E):
The circle moves sequentially one, two, three, four, ... spaces (each space is equal to half-a-side of the square boundary) in an ACW direction.

26. (C):
The number of sides of the figure reduces by one in each step.

27. (C):
Vertical and horizontal line segments are added to the figure alternately.

MODEL TEST PAPER

Answer Key

1. (B)	2. (C)	3. (A)	4. (C)	5. (A)	6. (D)	7. (C)	8. (B)	9. (B)	10. (A)
11. (B)	12. (B)	13. (B)	14. (B)	15. (C)	16. (A)	17. (C)	18. (D)	19. (A)	20. (D)
21. (B)	22. (D)	23. (B)	24. (A)	25. (A)	26. (A)	27. (C)	28. (C)	29. (B)	30. (A)
31. (B)	32. (B)	33. (A)	34. (B)	35. (C)	36. (B)	37. (A)	38. (C)	39. (B)	40. (A)
41. (A)	42. (C)	43. (A)	44. (C)	45. (D)	46. (D)	47. (A)	48. (C)	49. (D)	50. (B)

SAMPLE OMR ANSWER SHEET

1. STUDENT NAME (IN ENGLISH CAPITAL LETTERS ONLY)

Students must write and darken the respective circles completely using HB Pencil only. Othewise their Answer Sheets will not be evaluated.

PERSONAL DETAILS

2. SCHOOL CODE

3. CLASS

4. SECTION

5. ROLL NO.

6. QUESTION PAPER SET

A ○
B ○
C ○
D ○

7. MOBILE NUMBER

8. GENDER

MALE ○
FEMALE ○

9. STREAM

(Only for Class XI and XII Students)

MATHEMATICS ○
BIOLOGY ○
OTHERS ○

MARK YOUR ANSWERS

1.	A B C D	26.	A B C D
2.	A B C D	27.	A B C D
3.	A B C D	28.	A B C D
4.	A B C D	29.	A B C D
5.	A B C D	30.	A B C D
6.	A B C D	31.	A B C D
7.	A B C D	32.	A B C D
8.	A B C D	33.	A B C D
9.	A B C D	34.	A B C D
10.	A B C D	35.	A B C D
11.	A B C D	36.	A B C D
12.	A B C D	37.	A B C D
13.	A B C D	38.	A B C D
14.	A B C D	39.	A B C D
15.	A B C D	40.	A B C D
16.	A B C D	41.	A B C D
17.	A B C D	42.	A B C D
18.	A B C D	43.	A B C D
19.	A B C D	44.	A B C D
20.	A B C D	45.	A B C D
21.	A B C D	46.	A B C D
22.	A B C D	47.	A B C D
23.	A B C D	48.	A B C D
24.	A B C D	49.	A B C D
25.	A B C D	50.	A B C D

Signature of the Student & Date of Examination

Signature of the Invigilator & Date of Examination

V&S Publishers, F-2/16 Ansari Road, Daryaganj, New Delhi-110002, ☎ 011-23240026-27
✉ info@vspublishers.com, 🌐 www.vspublishers.com